Logical Fallacies for Kids

Outsmart Bad Reasoning and Catch Silly Arguments!

Table of Contents

Introduction: Welcome to the World of Logical Fallacies!

Hi there! Did you know your brain is like a superhero? It helps you solve problems, win arguments, and figure out the truth. But even superheroes have weaknesses, and their brains sometimes fall for tricks and traps called logical fallacies.

What's a Logical Fallacy?

It's a fancy way of saying "bad thinking." Logical fallacies happen when arguments don't make sense, even if they sound like they do. They're like sneaky little tricks that confuse people. But don't worry — you're about to learn how to spot them like a pro!

Here's an example:

- Imagine your friend says, "If you don't share your candy, you're a bad person!"

- Wait a second … does not sharing candy really make someone bad? Nope! That's called a fallacy — a bad argument designed to make you feel guilty instead of thinking clearly.

Why Does This Happen?

Humans sometimes fall for fallacies because they're emotional, tired, or just trying to win an argument quickly. But you're smarter than that! By learning about these common mistakes, you'll know when someone's argument doesn't add up.

Why Should You Learn This?

- You'll Outsmart Tricky Arguments: No one will be able to fool you with silly thinking.

- You'll Be a Super Debater: Whether you're talking to friends, family, or anyone else, you'll always have the sharpest mind in the room.

- You'll See the Truth: Knowing what makes a good argument helps you understand the world better — and even helps you make smarter decisions!

How This Book Works

Each chapter in this book will teach you about one fallacy. You'll see funny examples, learn why the fallacy doesn't work, and get tips on how to avoid it. Plus, you'll get some practice so you can become a fallacy-detecting ninja!

Get Ready for a Brain Workout!

By the end of this book, you'll have a powerful new skill: the ability to think clearly, argue fairly, and spot bad reasoning from a mile away. You're about to become the hero of logical thinking — so, grab your cape (or just a comfy chair), and let's jump into the first fallacy!

Chapter 1–10: Everyday Arguments

Welcome to "Everyday Arguments!" This is where you'll learn about some sneaky tricks people use when they argue. Sometimes, people make mistakes like attacking someone instead of their idea or pretending there are only two choices. But don't worry — you'll learn how to spot these mistakes and handle them like a pro. Let's get started and have some fun learning!

Chapter 1: The Ad Hominem Fallacy

What Is It?

The Ad Hominem fallacy happens when someone ignores an idea and instead attacks the person who said it.

Here's an example:

- **Kid 1:** "Eating veggies makes you healthy!"

- **Kid 2:** "What do you know? You didn't even eat broccoli yesterday!"

See the problem? Instead of thinking about the idea (*are veggies healthy?*), Kid 2 attacks Kid 1 (*you didn't eat broccoli*). That's Ad Hominem—a way to dodge the idea by pointing fingers.

Why Is This a Mistake?

Whether Kid 1 eats broccoli or not doesn't change if veggies are healthy. The idea is what matters, not the person saying it.

Think of it like this:

- **Idea:** Eating veggies makes you healthy.

- **Person:** Didn't eat broccoli yesterday.

- The person and the idea are *not* the same thing! The truth of the idea doesn't depend on who said it.

Why Do People Do This?

Sometimes, humans get mad or just want to win an argument, so they attack the person instead of thinking about the idea. It's like yelling, "Your shoes are ugly!" during a game of tag — totally unrelated and not helpful.

How to Avoid This Mistake

1. Listen to the idea. Forget about who said it—just think about whether the idea is true.

2. Ask yourself: "Would this idea still be true if someone else said it?"

3. Don't get personal. When you argue back, talk about the *idea*, not the person.

Practice Example

Let's try!

- Your friend says: "Reading every day makes you smarter."

- Instead of saying: "What do you know? You watch cartoons all day!"

- Ask yourself: "Hmm... is it true that reading makes people smarter?"

How to Handle Ad Hominem

If someone attacks you instead of your idea, don't worry! Here's what you can say:

1. **Bring the focus back:** "That's about me, but what do you think about the idea?"

2. **Make it look silly:** "Wow, I must have a strong idea if the only thing to argue about is me!"

3. **Invite them back to the topic:** "Okay, let's leave the personal stuff and talk about the idea instead."

4. **Use humor:** "Cool! Now that we've talked about me, can we talk about the actual point?"

Remember This:

Attacking the person is like throwing spaghetti at the wall — messy and pointless. Instead, stick to the idea, and you'll always be one step closer to the truth.

Chapter 2: The Straw Man Fallacy

What Is It?

The Straw Man fallacy happens when someone changes what you said to make it sound silly, extreme, or wrong, and then argues against that fake version of your idea.

Here's an Example:

- Kid 1: "I think we should play soccer."

- Kid 2: "Oh, so you hate all other sports now?"

Can you tell why this doesn't work? Kid 1 never said they hated other sports, but Kid 2 twisted the idea to make it sound extreme.

Why Is This a Mistake?

It's not fair to argue against something a person didn't actually say. Instead of listening to their real idea, you're arguing with a fake version of it —a "straw man." This doesn't help anyone understand the truth.

Why Do People Do This?

- It's easier to argue against a fake, exaggerated idea.

- They might not fully understand the real argument.

- They want to make their point seem stronger.

How to Avoid This Mistake:

1. Listen carefully to the other person's real idea.

2. Ask questions to make sure you understand: "Are you saying [the idea]?"

3. Respond to the real idea, not a twisted version of it.

Practice Example:

Let's try!

- Friend: "I think we should eat more fruit."

- Instead of saying: "Oh, so you think we should never eat cookies again?"

- Try saying: "Why do you think eating more fruit is a good idea?"

How to Handle the Straw Man Fallacy:

If someone twists your words, here's what you can say:

1. "That's not what I said. Let me explain what I actually meant."

2. "You're changing my words. Let's talk about my real idea instead."

3. "Here's what I really meant—can we focus on that?"

Remember This:

Arguing with a fake version of someone's idea is like fighting a shadow — it's pointless. Stick to the real idea to have a fair and helpful conversation.

Chapter 3: The False Dilemma Fallacy

What Is It?

The False Dilemma fallacy happens when someone makes it seem like there are only two choices, even though there are more options. It's like saying, "You can only have chocolate or vanilla," when there's a whole freezer of ice cream flavors!

Here's an Example:

- Kid 1: "You can either do your homework or never succeed!"

- Kid 2: "Wait, can't I do my homework and still have fun?"

Kid 1 is pretending there are only two choices, but Kid 2 shows that life isn't always so black and white.

Why Is This a Mistake?

Life is full of possibilities, and pretending there are only two choices can make people feel trapped or rushed into making the wrong decision. It's unfair and oversimplifies the situation.

Why Do People Do This?

- They want to make their choice seem better by ignoring other options.

- They don't take time to think about all the possibilities.

- They might want to pressure you into picking a side.

How to Avoid This Mistake

1. Ask, "Are these really the only two choices, or are there more?"

2. Take a moment to explore other ideas or solutions.

3. Don't let anyone rush you into deciding between two things if there might be more options.

Practice Example

Let's try!

- Kid 1: "You can either eat broccoli or go to bed hungry!"

- You: "Wait, what about eating something else, like carrots?"

How to Handle the False Dilemma Fallacy

If someone says you only have two choices, try this:

1. **Point Out Other Options:** "I don't think those are the only choices. Let's look at more ideas."

2. **Ask Questions:** "Why do you think it has to be just this or that?"

3. **Suggest a Middle Ground:** "How about we try both? Or something in between?"

Remember This:

The world isn't just black and white—it's full of colors and possibilities! Don't let someone force you into a choice when there might be lots of other options waiting to be discovered.

Chapter 4: The Bandwagon Fallacy

What Is It?

The Bandwagon fallacy happens when someone says something must be good, right, or true just because a lot of people like it or do it. It's like saying, "Everyone is jumping on this wagon, so it must be the best wagon ever!" But just because something is popular doesn't mean it's the right choice for you.

Here's an Example:

- Kid 1: "Everyone has these shoes, so they must be the best!"

- Kid 2: "Just because everyone has them doesn't mean they're the best for me."

See what's happening? Kid 1 is assuming the shoes are the best simply because they're popular. But Kid 2 knows that being popular doesn't always mean something is good or the right choice for everyone.

Why Is This a Mistake?

Popularity doesn't equal quality. Just because something is popular doesn't mean it's the best choice for you. Crowds can be wrong, and what's right for others might not be right for you. It's important to think for yourself instead of following what everyone else is doing.

Why Do People Do This?

- They want to fit in and be like everyone else.
- They think, "If everyone likes it, it must be great."
- They feel safer following the crowd instead of making their own choice.

How to Avoid This Mistake

1. **Think for Yourself:** Ask, "Do I actually like this, or do I just want to fit in?"

2. **Look for Reasons:** Ask, "Why is this popular? Is it actually good, or do people just think it is?"

3. **Be Brave:** It's okay to make your own choices, even if they're different from the crowd.

Practice Example

Let's try!

- Kid 1: "Everyone in my class says this video game is the best, so it must be!"

- You: "Maybe it's fun, but I want to check out reviews and see if it's something I'd like too."

How to Handle the Bandwagon Fallacy

If someone tries to convince you to follow the crowd, here's what you can say:

1. **Question It:** "Just because everyone's doing it, does that make it the best choice?"

2. **Be Confident:** "I don't need to follow the crowd to make a good decision."

3. **Suggest Thinking Together:** "Let's figure out if it's actually good instead of just popular."

Remember This:

It's okay to be different! What works for others might not work for you, and that's totally fine. Thinking for yourself makes you stronger and more independent, so don't let the crowd decide for you.

Chapter 5: The Appeal to Authority Fallacy

What Is It?

The Appeal to Authority fallacy happens when someone says something must be true just because an "important" or "smart" person said it — even if that person isn't an expert on the topic.

Here's an Example:

- Kid 1: "The best way to win a race is to wear shiny shoes."

- Kid 2: "Why do you think that?"

- Kid 1: "Because my cousin said so, and he's really cool!"

See the problem? Just because Kid 1's cousin is cool doesn't mean they know the best way to win a race. What matters is whether the idea itself makes sense, not who said it.

Why Is This a Mistake?

Good ideas and arguments should be based on facts, not just on who said them. Even smart or famous people can make mistakes or have opinions that aren't backed by proof. What matters most is whether the idea itself is true.

Why Do People Do This?

- They trust the person and assume they must be right.

- They think being smart, cool, or famous makes someone an expert.

- They don't stop to check if the person really knows what they're talking about.

How to Avoid This Mistake

1. Ask: "Is this person really an expert on this topic?"

2. Look for evidence: "Does their idea make sense on its own?"

3. Think for yourself: "Even if I like this person, is their argument logical and true?"

Practice Example

Let's try!

- Kid 1: "This app is the best because a famous YouTuber said so!"

- You: "That's cool, but let's look at reviews to see if it's really good."

How to Handle the Appeal to Authority Fallacy

If someone tells you to believe something just because an important person said it, try this:

1. **Ask Questions:** "How does this person know it's true? Are they an expert?"

2. **Look for Proof:** "Let's check if there's evidence to back this up."

3. **Be Polite but Firm:** "Even if this person is smart, I'd like to learn more about the idea itself."

Remember This:

It's okay to admire someone, but that doesn't mean everything they say is true. Always check the facts and think for yourself. The truth matters more than who said it!

Chapter 6: The Appeal to Emotion Fallacy

What Is It?

The Appeal to Emotion fallacy happens when someone tries to convince you by making you feel something — like guilt, fear, or sadness — rather than giving a good reason. Instead of explaining why their idea is right, they use emotions to push you to agree.

Here's an Example:

- Kid 1: "You should share your tablet because it'll make me happy!"

- Kid 2: "But being happy isn't a reason. Why do you need it?"

What's not adding up? Kid 1 isn't giving a real reason for sharing the tablet. Instead, they're using emotions to make Kid 2 feel bad so they'll give in.

Why Is This a Mistake?

Feelings are important, but they don't prove whether an argument is true or fair. A good argument should be based on reasons and facts, not just emotions. Using emotions might seem powerful, but it's not a fair way to have a discussion.

Why Do People Do This?

- They might not have a strong reason, so they rely on feelings to get their way.

- They know emotions like guilt or fear are hard to ignore.

- They may not realize they're trying to manipulate your feelings instead of explaining their point.

How to Avoid This Mistake

1. **Stay Calm:** Ask yourself, "Is this about facts or feelings?"

2. **Look for a Real Reason:** "Do they have a fair reason, or are they just trying to make me feel something?"

3. **Think Clearly:** Don't let your emotions stop you from making a smart decision.

Practice Example

Let's try!

- Kid 1: "You have to let me copy your homework, or I'll get in trouble!"

- You: "I don't want you to get in trouble, but copying isn't the right solution. Let's figure out how you can finish it yourself."

How to Handle the Appeal to Emotion Fallacy

If someone uses feelings to convince you, here's how you can respond:

1. **Acknowledge Their Feelings:** "I understand that you feel this way."

2. **Shift to the Real Issue:** "But let's talk about the actual reason why this matters."

3. **Be Kind but Firm:** "I care about how you feel, but I also want to make the right choice."

Remember This:

It's okay to care about other people's feelings, but don't let emotions replace good reasoning. Smart decisions are made by thinking clearly, even when feelings are involved.

All dogs are scary!"

Have you met every dog?

Chapter 7: The Hasty Generalization Fallacy

What Is It?

The Hasty Generalization fallacy happens when someone makes a big decision or assumption based on just one or a few examples. It's like saying, "I saw one rainy day, so it must rain every day!" without looking at the bigger picture.

Here's an Example:

- Kid 1: "I saw one scary dog, so all dogs must be mean!"

- Kid 2: "That's not true! Most dogs are friendly — you just saw one bad example."

See what's happening? Kid 1 is making a quick judgment about all dogs based on just one scary experience. But Kid 2 knows that one bad example doesn't tell the whole story.

Why Is This a Mistake?

It's unfair to decide something is true about everyone or everything based on just a small sample. You need more information before you can make a smart decision.

Why Do People Do This?

- They jump to conclusions instead of taking time to think.

- They let one bad (or good) experience shape their whole opinion.

- They don't stop to look at the bigger picture or more examples.

How to Avoid This Mistake

1. **Look for More Info:** Ask yourself, "Is this just one example, or do I know more about this?"

2. **Think Bigger:** "Does this really happen all the time, or is this just one situation?"

3. **Stay Open-Minded:** Be willing to admit you might need more facts before deciding.

Practice Example

Let's try!

- Kid 1: "The cafeteria food was bad today, so it must always be terrible!"

- You: "Maybe it's just bad today. Let's try it tomorrow and see if it's different."

How to Handle the Hasty Generalization Fallacy

If someone makes a quick judgment, here's what you can do:

1. **Ask for More Proof:** "Do you have more examples to back this up?"

2. **Point Out the Problem:** "That's just one example—you can't say it's true for everything."

3. **Encourage Patience:** "Let's take our time and look at more cases before deciding."

Remember This:

One example doesn't tell the whole story. Don't jump to conclusions — gather more facts and think carefully before making a big decision.

Chapter 8: The Slippery Slope Fallacy

What Is It?

The Slippery Slope fallacy happens when someone says that if one thing happens, it will lead to a chain of events that ends in something really bad—even if there's no good reason to think that will happen. It's like saying, "If you eat one cookie, you'll end up eating every cookie in the house!"

Here's an Example:

- Kid 1: "If we stay up late tonight, we'll never go to bed on time again!"

- Kid 2: "Why do you think that? Staying up late one time doesn't mean we'll never go to bed on time."

See why this doesn't fit? Kid 1 is assuming that one small action (staying up late) will lead to a huge problem without proof. Kid 2 knows that one choice doesn't always lead to a disaster.

Why Is This a Mistake?

Not every small action leads to a big chain reaction. Life isn't like a slippery slide where one small step means you're out of control. Decisions and events happen step by step, and one choice doesn't automatically mean the worst will happen.

Why Do People Do This?

- They're worried about the future and let their fears take over.

- They exaggerate to make their argument seem stronger.

- They might not realize they're skipping over all the steps in between.

How to Avoid This Mistake

1. **Take a Step Back:** Ask yourself, "Is this really going to lead to such a big problem?"

2. **Think About the Steps:** "What would actually have to happen to get from here to there?"

3. **Look for Proof:** "Do I have evidence that this will really happen?"

Practice Example

Let's try!

- Kid 1: "If we let people chew gum in class, soon everyone will bring snacks, and the classroom will be a mess!"

- You: "Chewing gum doesn't mean snacks will be allowed. Let's see if chewing gum actually causes problems first."

How to Handle the Slippery Slope Fallacy

If someone makes a wild claim about how one small thing will lead to disaster, try this:

1. **Ask for Proof:** "Why do you think this will happen?"

2. **Focus on the Present:** "Let's deal with what's happening right now instead of worrying about what might happen later."

3. **Stay Calm and Logical:** "One small choice doesn't mean everything will fall apart. Let's look at the facts."

Remember This:

Life doesn't slide out of control as easily as people might think. Instead of worrying about the worst-case scenario, focus on what's actually happening and take it one step at a time.

Chapter 9: The Red Herring Fallacy

What Is It?

The Red Herring fallacy happens when someone tries to distract you by changing the subject or bringing up something unrelated. It's like tossing a smelly fish (a "red herring") into the conversation to make you follow a new trail and forget the original point!

Here's an Example:

- Kid 1: "You didn't clean your room like you promised!"

- Kid 2: "Why are you always so mean to me?"

See the trick? Kid 1 wants to talk about cleaning the room, but Kid 2 changes the subject to avoid the issue. Instead of staying on topic, they bring up something unrelated to distract from the real conversation.

Why Is This a Mistake?

Good arguments stick to the point. Changing the subject might make someone forget the original issue, but it doesn't solve anything. It's like trying to win a race by running off the track — distracting, but not helpful.

Why Do People Do This?

- They don't have a good answer to the main topic.

- They want to confuse or distract the other person.

- They feel uncomfortable or nervous about the real issue.

How to Avoid This Mistake

1. **Stay Focused:** Ask, "Is this related to what we were talking about?"

2. **Bring It Back:** "Let's stick to the main point and talk about that first."

3. **Don't Get Distracted:** Think carefully about whether the new topic actually matters.

Practice Example:

Let's try!

- Kid 1: "You didn't share the markers during art class."

- Kid 2: "Well, you were late to class today!"

- You: "Being late isn't the same as sharing markers. Let's talk about sharing."

How to Handle the Red Herring Fallacy:

If someone tries to distract you, here's how you can respond:

1. **Point It Out:** "That's not what we were talking about. Let's get back to the topic."

2. **Ask for Focus:** "Can we stay on track and talk about this first?"

3. **Be Fair but Firm:** "We can talk about your point later, but let's finish this conversation first."

Remember This:

Stay focused! A good argument solves the real problem, not a different one. Don't let distractions lead you off track — stick to the topic and stay calm.

Chapter 10: The Circular Reasoning Fallacy

What Is It?

The Circular Reasoning fallacy happens when someone tries to prove their point by simply repeating it in a different way. It's like running in a circle — you don't get anywhere new! Instead of giving a real reason or proof, they just use the idea itself to explain why it's true.

Here's an Example:

- Kid 1: "This game is fun because it's enjoyable!"

- Kid 2: "But what makes it fun? You're just saying the same thing twice."

Kid 1 isn't giving a real reason for why the game is fun. They're just repeating the same idea using different words.

Why Is This a Mistake?

Good arguments need reasons that explain why something is true. If someone keeps going in circles, they're not adding anything new to the conversation. It might sound like they're making a point, but they're really just repeating themselves.

Why Do People Do This?

- They might not realize they're repeating their idea.

- They don't have a strong reason, so they keep saying the same thing in different ways.

- They hope you'll agree if they say it enough times.

How to Avoid This Mistake

1. **Ask Yourself:** "Does this explanation actually prove the idea, or is it just repeating it?"

2. **Look for Real Proof:** "What are the facts or reasons that back this up?"

3. **Take Your Time:** Don't rush to agree if the argument isn't clear or convincing.

Practice Example

Let's try!

- Kid 1: "We have to pick this team because it's the best!"

- You: "Why is it the best? Just saying it's the best doesn't explain why."

How to Handle the Circular Reasoning Fallacy

If someone keeps going in circles, here's how you can respond:

1. **Point It Out:** "You're just repeating the same idea. Can you explain it better?"

2. **Ask for More Details:** "What proof do you have for that?"

3. **Stay Calm:** "I want to understand your point, but you need to give a real reason, not just say the same thing again."

Remember This:

Good arguments move forward, not in circles. Always look for reasons and explanations that make sense and help you understand the idea better.

Chapter 11–20: Tricky Thinking

In this section, we'll explore some clever, but sneaky, ways people can make arguments that don't really work. These fallacies might seem tricky at first, but don't worry — you'll learn how to spot them and stay sharp. By the end of this section, you'll know how to handle everything from confusing questions to bad arguments about old traditions or new ideas.

Chapter 11: The Loaded Question Fallacy

What Is It?

The Loaded Question fallacy happens when someone asks a question that unfairly assumes something. No matter how you answer, it feels like you're agreeing to something you didn't mean to. It's like being asked, "Why did you eat all the cookies?" when you didn't eat any!

Here's an Example:

- Kid 1: "Why did you break my toy?"

- Kid 2: "Wait, I didn't break your toy! Let's figure out what happened."

Notice what's tricky here? Kid 1's question already assumes Kid 2 broke the toy, even though that might not be true. It's not fair to frame a question in a way that traps someone.

Why Is This a Mistake?

Loaded questions force people to defend themselves against something that might not even be true. It's unfair because the question assumes something bad, which can make it hard to give an honest answer.

Why Do People Do This?

- They want to trap you into admitting something.

- They think it's easier to win an argument by sneaking in an unfair assumption.

- They might not realize their question is unfair.

How to Avoid This Mistake

1. **Check Your Questions:** Ask yourself, "Am I assuming something that might not be true?"

2. **Be Fair:** Ask clear, honest questions that don't trap the other person.

3. **Stay Open-Minded:** Avoid jumping to conclusions before asking a question.

Practice Example

Let's try!

- Kid 1: "Why are you always mean to me?"

- You: "That's not true. Let's talk about how we can be nicer to each other."

How to Handle the Loaded Question Fallacy

If someone asks you an unfair question, here's what you can do:

1. **Don't Answer Right Away:** "Wait, I don't agree with the way you're asking that."

2. **Challenge the Assumption:** "I don't think that's true. Let's figure out what really happened."

3. **Ask for a Fair Question:** "Can you ask that in a way that doesn't assume I did something wrong?"

Remember This:

You don't have to answer unfair questions. It's okay to point out when someone is making an assumption. Honest conversations start with fair questions, so stay calm and keep the focus on the truth.

SEPARATE CHANCES

Each roll is RANDOM

"The chance stays the same every time!"

Chapter 12: The Gambler's Fallacy

What Is It?

The Gambler's Fallacy happens when someone thinks that what happened before can change what will happen next, even if the two events aren't connected. It's like saying, "The last three coin flips were heads, so the next one must be tails!" But each coin flip is a new chance, and the past flips don't change the odds.

Here's an Example:

- Kid 1: "This coin landed on heads five times in a row, so it has to be tails next!"

- Kid 2: "Nope! The coin still has the same chance to land on heads or tails every time."

See the mistake? Kid 1 is letting the past flips affect their thinking, even though each flip is random and doesn't depend on the last one.

Why Is This a Mistake?

Each event, like flipping a coin or rolling a die, is separate from the ones before it. What happened in the past doesn't change what will happen next. Thinking otherwise can lead to wrong predictions and decisions.

Why Do People Do This?

- They see patterns and think they must mean something.

- They hope they can predict what will happen next.

- They don't realize random events don't follow rules like "balancing out."

How to Avoid This Mistake

1. **Think Logically:** Remind yourself that each chance is separate.

2. **Don't Be Tricked by Patterns:** Just because something happened before doesn't mean it changes the next outcome.

3. **Focus on the Odds:** Look at the real chance of something happening.

Practice Example

Let's try!

- Kid 1: "I've lost five games in a row, so I'm definitely going to win the next one!"

- You: "Winning or losing depends on how you play, not on the last five games."

How to Handle the Gambler's Fallacy

If someone makes this mistake, here's how you can help:

1. **Explain It:** "Each chance is its own thing. What happened before doesn't change what happens next."

2. **Break It Down:** "If the odds are 50/50, they stay the same no matter what happened before."

3. **Stay Patient:** Help them see that patterns in random events don't really mean anything.

Remember This:

Random things don't follow rules like 'balancing out.' Each time is a brand-new chance, so don't let what happened before make you think it changes what comes next.

Chapter 13: The Appeal to Tradition Fallacy

What Is It?

The Appeal to Tradition fallacy happens when someone says something is the best or the right way to do things just because it's been done that way for a long time. It's like saying, "We've always done it this way, so we can't change!" But just because something is old doesn't mean it's the best choice now.

Here's an Example:

- Kid 1: "We always play tag at recess, so we can't play anything else."

- Kid 2: "Why not? Trying a new game could be fun!"

See the problem? Kid 1 is using tradition (always playing tag) as a reason to avoid trying something new. But just because they've always played tag doesn't mean it's the only or best option.

Why Is This a Mistake?

Tradition can be nice, but it's not always the best reason for making decisions. Times change, and new ideas might be better than old ones. If you stick to something just because it's "always been done," you might miss out on better or more exciting choices.

Why Do People Do This?

- They feel safe or comfortable with the way things have always been.

- They don't want to think about new ideas or changes.

- They think "old" automatically means "better" or "right."

How to Avoid This Mistake

1. **Ask Why:** "Why do we do it this way? Is it the best way, or just the old way?"

2. **Be Open to Change:** "Could a new idea work better?"

3. **Think for Yourself:** Don't assume something is right just because it's a tradition.

Practice Example

Let's try!

- Kid 1: "We've always eaten pizza on Fridays, so we can't try something new!"

- You: "Pizza is great, but why not try tacos this Friday and see if we like it?"

How to Handle the Appeal to Tradition Fallacy

If someone says you should do something just because it's a tradition, here's how you can respond:

1. **Question It:** "Just because we've always done it this way, does that mean it's the best way?"

2. **Suggest Something New:** "What if we try a new idea and see how it works?"

3. **Find a Balance:** "We can keep traditions we like, but it's also okay to try new things!"

Remember This:

Traditions can be fun and meaningful, but they aren't always the best reason to make a decision. It's okay to ask questions, think about new ideas, and even start your own traditions. Being open to change helps you grow and learn!

Chapter 14: The Sunk Cost Fallacy

What Is It?

The Sunk Cost fallacy happens when someone keeps doing something just because they've already spent time, money, or effort on it — even if it's not worth it anymore. It's like saying, "I've already eaten half this burned pizza, so I have to eat the rest!" when you could just stop and eat something better.

Here's an Example:

- Kid 1: "I've already spent an hour building this tower, so I can't stop now, even though it keeps falling!"

- Kid 2: "Maybe it's better to start over and build something else that works better."

See the mistake? Kid 1 is sticking with the tower just because they've already spent time on it, even though it might be smarter to start fresh.

Why Is This a Mistake?

Sometimes, we feel like we have to keep going because of what we've already done. But what's already spent — time, effort, or money — can't be changed. Instead of focusing on the past, it's better to think about what will work best moving forward.

Why Do People Do This?

- They don't want to feel like their time or effort was wasted.

- They're too focused on the past to think about what's best for the future.

- They hope things will magically get better if they just keep going.

How to Avoid This Mistake

1. **Think Ahead:** Ask yourself, "Will continuing this make things better, or am I just doing it because of the past?"

2. **Let Go of the Past:** Remember, what's done is done — you can't change it.

3. **Focus on the Future:** Choose what's best for you now, even if it means starting over.

Practice Example

Let's try!

- Kid 1: "I've already spent all my allowance on this broken toy, so I have to keep trying to fix it."

- You: "Maybe it's better to stop and save for something new that actually works."

How to Handle the Sunk Cost Fallacy

If someone is stuck because of what they've already spent, here's what you can say:

1. "What's the best choice moving forward, even if it means letting go of the past?"

2. "It's okay to start over. You'll get better results in the end."

3. "Think about what will make you happiest now, not what you've already done."

Remember This

Don't get stuck because of what you've already spent. Focus on what will help you now and in the future — sometimes starting fresh is the smartest choice.

Chapter 15: The Middle Ground Fallacy

What Is It?

The Middle Ground fallacy happens when someone says the truth must be somewhere in the middle of two sides, even if one side is completely wrong. It's like saying, "If one person says the Earth is flat and another says it's round, it must be half-round and half-flat!"

Here's an Example:

- Kid 1: "We should have homework every single day."

- Kid 2: "We shouldn't have any homework at all."

- Kid 3: "Maybe we should have homework only on weekends."

See the problem? Kid 3 assumes the middle ground is the best choice, but that doesn't mean it's the right one. Sometimes, one side is better than the other!

Why Is This a Mistake?

Just because two sides disagree doesn't mean the answer is in the middle. The truth depends on the facts, not on picking something halfway between two opinions.

Why Do People Do This?

- They think being "fair" means meeting in the middle.

- They don't want to upset anyone, so they compromise even when it doesn't make sense.

- They assume both sides must have equal value.

How to Avoid This Mistake

1. **Look at the Facts:** Ask, "Which side is supported by evidence?"

2. **Be Brave:** It's okay to choose one side if it's the better choice.

3. **Think Clearly:** Don't assume the middle is automatically the best answer.

Practice Example

Let's try!

- Kid 1: "I say we should stay at recess all day."

- Kid 2: "I say we shouldn't have recess at all."

- You: "Let's see what's fair based on the rules instead of just picking the middle."

How to Handle the Middle Ground Fallacy

If someone assumes the middle is always right, here's how you can respond:

1. **Focus on the Facts:** "Let's figure out which idea actually makes sense."

2. **Ask Questions:** "Does the middle choice really solve the problem?"

3. **Stay Fair:** "The middle isn't always best. Let's look at what works instead."

Remember This:

Being in the middle doesn't make something right. The truth depends on the facts, not just picking a spot between two sides.

Chapter 16: The Cherry Picking Fallacy

What Is It?

The Cherry Picking fallacy happens when someone only uses the facts that support their argument and ignores the rest. It's like saying, "This fruit salad is all strawberries!" when you're ignoring the apples, bananas, and grapes.

Here's an Example:

- Kid 1: "This game is the best because it has cool characters!"

- Kid 2: "But what about the bad controls and boring levels?"

Kid 1 is only focusing on one good thing and ignoring the rest. A fair argument should look at all the facts, not just the ones you like.

Why Is This a Mistake?

Focusing on only part of the story doesn't give the full picture. Ignoring important facts can make your argument unfair or misleading.

Why Do People Do This?

- They want their argument to look stronger than it really is.

- They don't want to talk about the bad parts of their idea.

- They think no one will notice the missing information.

How to Avoid This Mistake

1. **Look at Everything:** Ask, "What other facts might I be ignoring?"

2. **Be Honest:** Include both the good and the bad when making your argument.

3. **Think Critically:** Don't let someone convince you with just half the story.

Practice Example

Let's try!

- Kid 1: "This new show is amazing because the main character is funny!"

- You: "That's true, but is the story interesting too? Let's look at the whole picture."

How to Handle the Cherry Picking Fallacy

If someone is only using part of the facts, here's how you can respond:

1. **Ask for the Rest:** "What about the things you didn't mention? Let's look at those too."

2. **Point Out the Problem:** "You're only talking about the good parts, but what about the bad ones?"

3. **Be Fair:** "It's important to look at everything, not just the parts we like."

Remember This:

A fair argument includes all the facts. Don't just pick the "cherries" — look at the whole story to make a smart decision.

Chapter 17: The Appeal to Nature Fallacy

What Is It?

The Appeal to Nature fallacy happens when someone says something is good or right just because it's "natural," or bad just because it's "unnatural." It's like saying, "This candy is bad for you because it isn't made from plants!" without looking at whether the candy is healthy or not.

Here's an Example:

- Kid 1: "You shouldn't use a calculator—it's not natural!"

- Kid 2: "But calculators help solve math problems faster. Isn't that what matters?"

Can you tell what's wrong here? Kid 1 is focusing on whether the calculator is "natural" instead of whether it's useful or helpful.

Why Is This a Mistake?

Just because something is natural doesn't mean it's good, and just because something is unnatural doesn't mean it's bad. For example, natural things like poison ivy can be harmful, while "unnatural" things like medicine can help save lives.

Why Do People Do This?

- They think natural things are always better because they come from nature.

- They want to avoid things that seem strange or unfamiliar.

- They assume "natural" and "good" mean the same thing.

How to Avoid This Mistake

1. **Ask Questions:** "Is this natural thing actually good, or am I just assuming it is?"

2. **Think About the Purpose:** "Does it work or help, whether it's natural or not?"

3. **Focus on the Facts:** Look at what makes something good or bad, not just whether it's natural.

Practice Example

Let's try!

- Kid 1: "This snack is healthier because it's natural."

- You: "Let's check the ingredients and see if it's really good for us."

How to Handle the Appeal to Nature Fallacy

If someone says something is good or bad because of how "natural" it is, you can respond by:

1. **Questioning It:** "What does natural have to do with whether it's good or bad?"

2. **Looking for Proof:** "Let's check if it's actually helpful or harmful."

3. **Staying Open-Minded:** "Natural doesn't always mean good, and unnatural doesn't always mean bad."

Remember This:

What matters is whether something is helpful, safe, or effective—not whether it's natural. Look at the facts, not just the label.

Chapter 18: The Appeal to Consequences Fallacy

What Is It?

The Appeal to Consequences fallacy happens when someone says an idea must be true or false based on whether the result is good or bad, instead of looking at the facts. It's like saying, "This can't be true because I don't like what would happen if it is!"

Here's an Example:

- Kid 1: "If we don't win the soccer game, Coach will be disappointed, so we have to win!"

- Kid 2: "Coach might be disappointed, but that doesn't change whether we win or lose."

Kid 1 is focusing on the consequences of losing instead of the reality of the situation.

Why Is This a Mistake?

Good arguments are based on facts, not just on how the outcome makes you feel. The truth doesn't change just because you like or dislike what it leads to.

Why Do People Do This?

- They want to avoid bad outcomes.

- They think emotions or consequences are more important than the facts.

- They might not realize they're letting feelings influence their thinking.

How to Avoid This Mistake

1. **Focus on Facts:** Ask, "Is this true, even if the result isn't what I want?"

2. **Separate Feelings from Truth:** "How I feel about the outcome doesn't change the facts."

3. **Think Clearly:** Don't let fear or hope distract you from the truth.

Practice Example

Let's try!

- Kid 1: "We can't lose this game because it would ruin my day!"

- You: "Losing might be disappointing, but let's focus on playing our best."

How to Handle the Appeal to Consequences Fallacy

If someone lets the result affect how they think, try this

1. **Ask Questions:** "Does the result change whether this is true or false?"

2. **Bring Back the Facts:** "Let's focus on what's real, not just how we feel about it."

3. **Encourage Clear Thinking:** "The outcome matters, but so does figuring out the truth."

Remember This:

The truth stays the same, even if you don't like the results. Focus on facts first, and then think about what to do next.

Chapter 19: The Personal Incredulity Fallacy

What Is It?

The Personal Incredulity fallacy happens when someone says something can't be true just because they don't understand it or find it hard to believe. It's like saying, "I don't get how this works, so it must be fake!"

Here's an Example:

- Kid 1: "How can planes fly? They're so heavy! That can't be real."

- Kid 2: "Just because you don't understand it doesn't mean it's not real. Planes fly because of science and engines!"

See the problem? Kid 1 thinks planes can't fly just because they don't understand how it works. But not understanding something doesn't make it untrue.

Why Is This a Mistake?

The world is full of things we might not fully understand, but that doesn't mean they aren't real. Instead of relying on what you know, it's better to learn more and find out the facts.

Why Do People Do This?

- They feel confused and think something can't be true because they don't get it.

- They assume that if they can't explain it, no one can.

- They might be too quick to dismiss new ideas.

How to Avoid This Mistake

1. **Be Curious:** Ask, "What can I learn about this to understand it better?"

2. **Stay Open-Minded:** "Just because I don't understand it doesn't mean it's wrong."

3. **Look for Answers:** Research or ask questions to find out more about the topic.

Practice Example

Let's try!

- Kid 1: "How can birds fly? That doesn't make sense!"

- You: "Birds can fly because of their wings and how they push against the air. Let's learn more about it together!"

How to Handle the Personal Incredulity Fallacy

If someone says something isn't true because they don't understand it, try this:

1. **Encourage Learning:** "Let's figure out how it works together."

2. **Point Out the Problem:** "Just because you don't get it doesn't mean it's not real."

3. **Stay Positive:** "It's okay to not know everything—we can always learn more!"

Remember This:

Not understanding something doesn't make it untrue. The world is full of amazing things, so stay curious and keep learning!

Chapter 20: The Appeal to Novelty Fallacy

What Is It?

The Appeal to Novelty fallacy happens when someone says something must be better or true just because it's new. It's like saying, "This brand-new toy is the best because it just came out!" But new doesn't always mean better — it's important to look at the facts.

Here's an Example:

- Kid 1: "This new phone is the best because it's the newest model!"

- Kid 2: "But is it really better? Let's check what it can do."

Kid 1 is assuming the phone is the best just because it's new, but Kid 2 knows that being new doesn't automatically make something the best.

Why Is This a Mistake?

Not everything new is better, just like not everything old is bad. New things can have problems, and sometimes older things work just as well—or even better! It's important to check if the new thing is actually an improvement.

Why Do People Do This?

- They get excited about new things because they seem cool or different.

- They assume anything new must be better than what came before.

- They want to keep up with trends and don't want to feel left out.

How to Avoid This Mistake

1. **Check the Details:** Ask, "What makes this new thing better?"

2. **Think Before You Decide:** "Is this really better, or does it just look new and shiny?"

3. **Compare Carefully:** Look at what the new thing can do versus the old one.

Practice Example

Let's try!

- Kid 1: "This new game must be awesome because it just came out!"

- You: "Let's read some reviews to see if it's actually fun to play."

How to Handle the Appeal to Novelty Fallacy

If someone says something is better just because it's new, here's how you can respond:

1. **Ask Questions:** "What makes this better than the old one?"

2. **Look for Evidence:** "Let's check if it's actually improved or just new."

3. **Be Open-Minded:** "New doesn't always mean better — let's find out if it's worth it."

Remember This:

New things can be cool, but they're not always better. What matters is if it works well or is actually improved — not just because it's the newest thing. Take your time to decide before getting too excited about what's new!

Chapter 21–30: Sneaky Tricks

This section is all about tricky ways people try to win arguments or convince others, even when their ideas don't really make sense. These fallacies are like little traps that can confuse you if you're not careful. Don't worry — you'll learn how to spot and handle them, so you can stay one step ahead!

Chapter 21: The No True Scotsman Fallacy

What Is It?

The No True Scotsman fallacy happens when someone says, "You're not part of the group because you don't act the way I think you should." It's like saying, "No real fans of this team would cheer for the other side," even though some fans might!

Here's an Example:

- Kid 1: "No true gamer likes puzzle games."

- Kid 2: "But I'm a gamer, and I like puzzle games!"

- Kid 1: "Well, then you're not a true gamer!"

Kid 1 is changing the definition of "gamer" to make their argument work, instead of accepting that different people can have different tastes.

Why Is This a Mistake?

It's not fair to change the rules about who belongs in a group just to win an argument. People in the same group can be different and have their own ideas — and that's totally okay!

Why Do People Do This?

- They want their group to seem better or more special.

- They don't like admitting that other opinions exist.

- They believe changing the rules will make their argument seem right.

How to Avoid This Mistake

1. **Be Open-Minded:** Accept that people in a group can have different ideas.

2. **Stick to the Facts:** Don't change definitions just to win an argument.

3. **Respect Others:** Let people define their own interests or identities.

Practice Example

Let's try!

- Kid 1: "No true soccer player would ever play video games!"

- You: "That's not fair. Lots of great soccer players also like video games!"

How to Handle the No True Scotsman Fallacy

If someone tries to exclude you or others with this fallacy, say:

1. "Why does someone have to fit your definition to be part of the group?"

2. "People can have different opinions and still belong to the same group."

3. "Let's focus on the actual topic instead of changing the rules."

Remember This:

Groups can have lots of different people with lots of different ideas. Changing the definition of a group just to win an argument isn't helpful.

Chapter 22: The Texas Sharpshooter Fallacy

What Is It?

The Texas Sharpshooter fallacy happens when someone only pays attention to the facts that make their argument look good and ignores everything else — kind of like drawing a target around the spots where their darts already landed to make it look like they hit the bullseye!

Here's an Example:

- Kid 1: "Our class is the best because we won three awards this year!"

- Kid 2: "But other classes won awards too, and some of them won even more."

Kid 1 is only looking at the good parts and ignoring the rest of the facts.

Why Is This a Mistake?

Only looking at facts that make you seem right doesn't tell the whole story. A good argument needs to include all the facts, even the ones that don't agree with you.

Why Do People Do This?

- They want to make their argument look stronger.

- They don't want to deal with information that disagrees with them.

- They think no one will notice what they left out.

How to Avoid This Mistake

1. **Look at Everything:** Don't ignore facts that don't fit your idea.

2. **Be Honest:** Share the full story, not just the parts that help you.

3. **Ask Questions:** Check if someone is leaving out important information.

Practice Example

Let's try!

- Kid 1: "This snack is the healthiest because it has fruit in it!"

- You: "But it's also full of sugar. Let's look at the whole picture."

How to Handle the Texas Sharpshooter Fallacy

If someone focuses only on certain facts, say:

1. "What about the other information you're leaving out?"

2. "Let's look at all the facts, not just the ones that fit your idea."

3. "It's important to be fair and honest about everything."

Remember This:

Good arguments include the whole story, not just the parts that look good. Always ask for the full picture before deciding what's true.

Chapter 23: The Survivorship Bias Fallacy

What Is It?

The Survivorship Bias fallacy happens when someone only looks at successes and ignores failures. It's like saying, "Anyone can become a famous singer if they practice every day!" without thinking about all the people who practiced hard but never became famous.

Here's an Example:

- Kid 1: "If we practice every day, we'll win the championship because last year's team did!"

- Kid 2: "But what about all the teams that practiced just as much and didn't win?"

What doesn't seem right? Kid 1 is only looking at the team that won and ignoring the others who worked just as hard but didn't succeed.

Why Is This a Mistake?

Focusing only on the winners doesn't give you the full story. Success can teach you valuable lessons, but failures are just as important because they show what didn't work. Ignoring failures might make success seem easier than it really is.

Why Do People Do This?

- Success stories are exciting and easy to remember.

- They want to feel hopeful and inspired, so they ignore failures.

- They assume that copying a winner's actions will guarantee success.

How to Avoid This Mistake

1. **Ask About Failures:** "What happened to the people who tried this and didn't succeed?"

2. **Look at the Bigger Picture:** Success is great, but it's only part of the story.

3. **Be Realistic:** Remember that success isn't always guaranteed, even with hard work.

Practice Example

Let's try!

- Kid 1: "All the best basketball players practiced every day, so if I practice, I'll be a pro too!"

- You: "Practice is important, but not everyone who practices becomes a pro. Let's focus on getting better for now."

How to Handle the Survivorship Bias Fallacy

If someone is only focusing on successes, try this:

1. **Ask Questions:** "What about the people who did the same thing but didn't succeed?"

2. **Show the Whole Picture:** "Success stories are great, but failures can teach us, too."

3. **Be Encouraging:** "You can still work hard and do your best, but remember that success takes more than just copying others."

Remember This

Success stories are inspiring, but they're not the full story. Don't forget to learn from failures—they can teach you just as much (or even more!) about how to improve and make smarter choices.

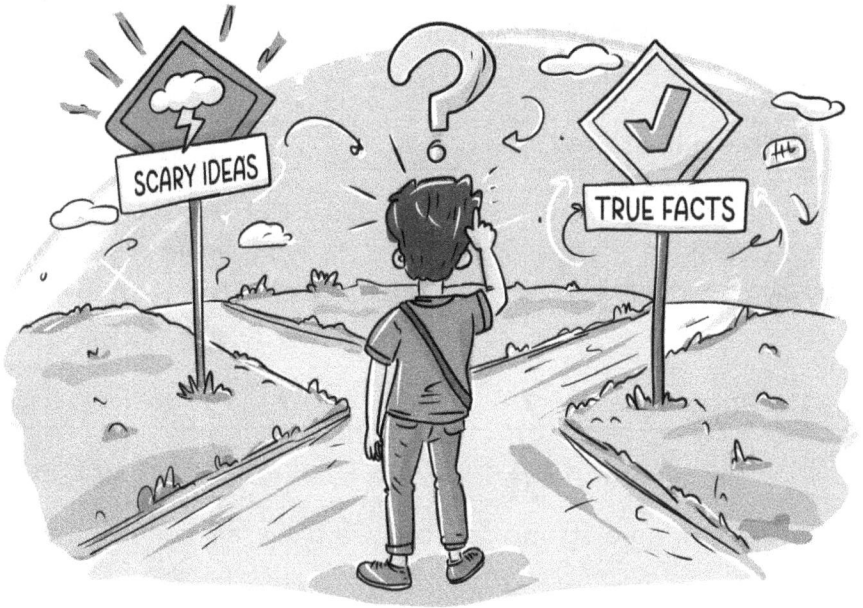

Chapter 24: The Scare Tactic Fallacy

What Is It?

The Scare Tactic fallacy happens when someone tries to scare you into agreeing with them instead of giving good reasons. It's like saying, "If you don't eat your vegetables, you'll never grow tall!" Scary statements might make you feel worried, but they're not always based on facts.

Here's an Example:

- Kid 1: "If you don't join the soccer team, you'll have no friends!"

- Kid 2: "That's not true! I can still have friends even if I don't play soccer."

Can you tell what's wrong here? Kid 1 is using fear to convince Kid 2, instead of explaining why the soccer team is a good choice.

Why Is This a Mistake?

Fear might grab your attention, but it's not a good reason to make a decision. Scary claims don't always tell the whole truth, and they can push you into making a choice that isn't right for you.

Why Do People Do This?

- They think fear is the easiest way to get someone to agree.

- They don't have strong reasons, so they rely on making you worried.

- They might be scared themselves and want you to feel the same way.

How to Avoid This Mistake

1. **Stay Calm:** Don't let fear stop you from thinking clearly.

2. **Ask Questions:** "Is this fear based on facts, or is it just to scare me?"

3. **Look for Proof:** Make decisions based on good reasons, not just scary ones.

Practice Example

Let's try!

- Kid 1: "If you don't study super hard, you'll fail every test!"

- You: "I'll study because it helps me learn, not because I'm scared of failing."

How to Handle the Scare Tactic Fallacy

If someone tries to scare you into agreeing with them, say:

1. "Why do you think that will happen? Can you explain more?"

2. "I'm not going to decide based on fear—I want to know the real reasons."

3. "Scary doesn't always mean true. Let's look at the facts instead."

Remember This:

Fear can feel powerful, but it doesn't mean something is true. Take a deep breath, think carefully, and make decisions based on reasons, not just scary words.

Chapter 25: The Appeal to Personal Experience Fallacy

What Is It?

The Appeal to Personal Experience fallacy happens when someone says their own experience is proof of something being true for everyone. It's like saying, "This snack is the best because I like it!" Your experience is important, but it's not always enough to prove something for everyone.

Here's an Example:

- Kid 1: "I've never seen a shooting star, so they must not be real."

- Kid 2: "Just because you haven't seen one doesn't mean they don't exist."

Do you see the mix-up? Kid 1 is using their own experience to decide what's true, but Kid 2 knows that one person's experience isn't enough to prove something for everyone.

Why Is This a Mistake?

One person's experience is just a single piece of the puzzle. The world is big, and different people have different experiences. A good argument looks at more than just one person's point of view.

Why Do People Do This?

- They believe their own experience because it feels real to them.

- They think if something happened to them, it must happen to everyone.

- They don't always realize that other people's experiences might be different.

How to Avoid This Mistake

1. **Think Bigger:** Ask, "Could other people's experiences be different from mine?"

2. **Look for Evidence:** "What else can we learn about this beyond just my experience?"

3. **Stay Open-Minded:** Be willing to accept that your experience might not tell the whole story.

Practice Example

Let's try!

- Kid 1: "I've never gotten sick from not washing my hands, so it's not important."

- You: "Just because you haven't gotten sick doesn't mean it can't happen. Let's check what doctors say."

How to Handle the Appeal to Personal Experience Fallacy

If someone says their experience proves something, you can respond:

1. "Your experience is important, but it might not be true for everyone."

2. "Let's look at other people's experiences and see what they say."

3. "One story doesn't tell the whole truth—let's check the facts."

Remember This

Your experience matters, but it's not the whole picture. To understand something fully, you need to look at many experiences and facts, not just your own.

Great Puzzle Pieces   The Full Puzzle

Chapter 26: The Composition Fallacy

What Is It?

The Composition fallacy happens when someone assumes that if one part of something is true, it must be true for the whole thing. It's like saying, "This puzzle piece is blue, so the whole puzzle must be blue!"

Here's an Example:

- Kid 1: "My favorite player is on this team, so the whole team must be amazing!"

- Kid 2: "But what about the rest of the players? One person doesn't make a whole team great."

What's the issue here? Kid 1 is judging the whole team based on just one player, but Kid 2 knows you have to look at everything to decide.

Why Is This a Mistake?

One part of something doesn't always tell you about the whole. A good argument looks at all the parts together, not just one piece.

Why Do People Do This?

- They think the best part represents everything.

- They don't take the time to look at all the details.

- They get excited about one thing and forget to check the rest.

How to Avoid This Mistake

1. **Look at the Whole Picture:** Don't judge the whole based on one piece.

2. **Ask Questions:** "What are the other parts like? Do they match this one?"

3. **Think Carefully:** Take your time to check all the details before deciding.

Practice Example

Let's try!

- Kid 1: "This book has a cool cover, so the whole story must be awesome!"

- You: "The cover is nice, but let's read a little to see if the story is good too."

How to Handle the Composition Fallacy

If someone judges the whole based on one part, you can say:

1. "That one part is great, but what about the rest?"

2. "Let's check all the pieces before we decide."

3. "One good piece doesn't mean the whole thing is amazing."

Remember This:

The best way to judge something is by looking at all the parts, not just one. Don't let one shiny piece trick you into thinking the whole thing is perfect!

Chapter 27: The Division Fallacy

What Is It?

The Division fallacy happens when someone thinks that what's true for the whole thing must also be true for every little part. It's like saying, "This cake is yummy, so every ingredient must taste yummy too!"

Here's an Example:

- Kid 1: "Our soccer team is the best, so every player must be the best too!"

- Kid 2: "Not every player has to be the best for the team to be great. It's about teamwork!"

Do you spot what's wrong? Kid 1 thinks every part of the team must be amazing just because the whole team is great, but Kid 2 knows that's not always true.

Why Is This a Mistake?

Sometimes the whole is great because of how the parts work together, not because every single part is perfect. Judging the pieces based on the whole can lead to wrong ideas.

Why Do People Do This?

- They think the greatness of the whole automatically applies to every part.

- They don't look at each part separately.

- They want to believe everything about the group is equally good.

How to Avoid This Mistake

1. **Look Closely:** Ask, "Does this part actually match the whole?"

2. **Check the Details:** Think about each piece individually.

3. **Think Clearly:** Remember, something can be great as a whole without every part being amazing.

Practice Example

Let's try!

- Kid 1: "This movie is awesome, so every single scene must be perfect!"

- You: "The movie is great, but maybe some parts are stronger than others."

How to Handle the Division Fallacy

If someone assumes the parts are just like the whole, you can say:

1. "Let's look at each part to see if it's the same as the whole."

2. "The group can be great without every part being perfect."

3. "What makes the whole special might be how the parts work together."

Remember This

Great things are often made up of different pieces, and not all of them have to be perfect. Always take a closer look at each part!

Chapter 28: The Appeal to Hypocrisy (Tu Quoque) Fallacy

What Is It?

The Appeal to Hypocrisy fallacy happens when someone tries to ignore the argument by saying, "You do the same thing!" It's like saying, "You can't tell me not to litter because you littered once too!"

Here's an Example:

- Kid 1: "You shouldn't eat so much candy—it's bad for you."

- Kid 2: "Why should I listen to you? You ate candy yesterday!"

What's off here? Kid 2 is ignoring Kid 1's advice by pointing out something Kid 1 did in the past. But just because someone else isn't perfect doesn't mean their advice is wrong.

Why Is This a Mistake?

This fallacy distracts from the real argument. Instead of focusing on whether the advice is good, it turns the conversation into pointing fingers, which doesn't solve anything.

Why Do People Do This?

- They try to avoid talking about the real issue.

- They think if they point out a mistake you made, they don't have to listen to your advice.

- It's easier to blame someone else than to think carefully about the argument.

How to Avoid This Mistake

1. **Focus on the Argument:** Ask, "Is the advice good, no matter who says it?"

2. **Don't Get Distracted:** Stick to the topic instead of talking about the person.

3. **Stay Fair:** Just because someone isn't perfect doesn't mean their argument isn't valid.

Practice Example

Let's try!

- Kid 1: "You should recycle more to help the planet."

- You: "Even if you forgot to recycle last week, that doesn't mean recycling isn't important."

How to Handle the Appeal to Hypocrisy Fallacy

If someone tries this fallacy, you can say:

1. "Let's focus on the idea, not what the other person did."

2. "Even if someone isn't perfect, their advice can still be helpful."

3. "It's not about who said it—it's about whether it's a good idea."

Remember This:

Pointing fingers doesn't solve anything. Focus on the idea itself and decide if it's good or not, no matter who said it.

Chapter 29: The Appeal to Pity Fallacy

What Is It?

The Appeal to Pity fallacy happens when someone tries to win an argument by making you feel sorry for them instead of giving good reasons. It's like saying, "You have to let me win this game because I had a bad day!"

Here's an Example:

- Kid 1: "I should get extra time on my homework because my dog was barking all night."

- Kid 2: "I'm sorry your dog kept you up, but we all have the same deadline."

Notice what's wrong? Kid 1 is asking for extra time not because of the homework but because of their situation. While it's okay to feel sympathy, it doesn't mean the rules should change.

Why Is This a Mistake?

Feeling bad for someone doesn't make their argument true. Sympathy is important, but it's not a reason to ignore facts or rules.

Why Do People Do This?

- They hope emotions will make you agree with them.

- They don't have strong reasons, so they use pity instead.

- They think making you feel sorry will help them get what they want.

How to Avoid This Mistake

1. **Be Kind but Fair:** Feel sympathy, but don't let it change the facts.

2. **Ask for Reasons:** "Why should we do this, other than feeling bad?"

3. **Stick to the Topic:** Focus on the issue, not the emotions.

Practice Example

Let's try!

- Kid 1: "You should trade snacks with me because I forgot mine at home."

- You: "I feel bad that you forgot your snack, but we need to make a fair trade."

How to Handle the Appeal to Pity Fallacy

If someone uses pity to convince you, try this:

1. "I understand how you feel, but we need to look at the facts too."

2. "Let's think about what's fair for everyone."

3. "Feeling bad for someone doesn't always mean they're right."

Remember This:

It's okay to feel sympathy, but emotions aren't a reason to ignore facts or make decisions. Be kind, but think clearly!

Chapter 30: The False Equivalence Fallacy

What Is It?

The False Equivalence fallacy happens when someone says two things are the same, even though they're very different. It's like saying, "Apples and oranges are the same because they're both fruits!" Sure, they're both fruits, but they're not the same in other ways — they taste different, look different, and grow in different places.

Here's an Example:

- Kid 1: "Getting a bad grade on a test is just as bad as failing the whole class!"

- Kid 2: "Not really! One bad grade can be fixed, but failing the whole class is a much bigger deal."

Can you see what's wrong here? Kid 1 is treating two very different things as if they're equal, but Kid 2 knows they're not the same.

Why Is This a Mistake?

When you treat two things as equal when they're not, it can confuse people and make your argument unfair. Real decisions and problems need to be looked at carefully to see what's really similar and what's not.

Why Do People Do This?

- They want to make their argument sound stronger by comparing it to something bigger or more serious.

- They don't take the time to notice the differences between the two things.

- They might not realize they're comparing two things that aren't truly alike.

How to Avoid This Mistake

1. **Look Closely:** Ask, "Are these two things really the same, or are they just a little similar?"

2. **Be Honest:** Think about the differences as well as the similarities.

3. **Explain Clearly:** Make sure your argument is based on fair comparisons.

Practice Example

Let's try!

- Kid 1: "Not finishing my chores is just as bad as breaking a rule!"

- You: "They're both important, but breaking a rule is usually more serious than forgetting a chore."

How to Handle the False Equivalence Fallacy

If someone tries to compare two things that aren't really the same, you can say:

1. "They're not the same — here's why."

2. "Let's look at how these two things are different."

3. "It's not fair to compare them if they're not alike in important ways."

Remember This:

Not all things that seem similar are actually the same. Look closely, think carefully, and make sure your comparisons are fair and true!

Chapter 31 – 40: Deceptive Arguments

Let's explore tricky ways people try to win arguments or make their ideas seem right, even when they're not! These fallacies may sound convincing at first, but once you learn to spot them, they're easy to see through. Get ready to uncover these sneaky tricks and learn how to think clearly and fairly.

Chapter 31: The Genetic Fallacy

What Is It?

The Genetic Fallacy happens when someone says an idea is good or bad just because of where it came from, not because of what it's about. It's like saying, "This game must be bad because it's made by a small company!" The origin of something doesn't always tell you if it's good or bad.

Here's an Example:

- Kid 1: "That toy can't be fun—it's from a store I don't like!"

- Kid 2: "But have you tried it? The store doesn't decide if the toy is fun or not."

What's wrong here? Kid 1 is judging the toy based on where it came from instead of whether it's actually fun.

Why Is This a Mistake?

Where something comes from doesn't always tell you how good or bad it is. Judging ideas or things based only on their source can make you miss out on something great—or believe in something that isn't.

Why Do People Do This?

- They assume the source tells the whole story.

- They want to quickly decide if something is good or bad without looking deeper.

- They trust or dislike certain sources and let that decide for them.

How to Avoid This Mistake

1. **Focus on the Idea:** Ask, "Is this thing good or bad because of what it is, not where it came from?"

2. **Be Curious:** Learn more about the idea itself, not just its source.

3. **Give Things a Chance:** Don't dismiss something without checking it out first.

Practice Example

Let's try!

- Kid 1: "That book can't be good—it's from the library's old section!"

- You: "Let's read a little and see if the story is fun, no matter where it's from."

How to Handle the Genetic Fallacy

If someone says an idea is bad just because of where it came from, you can respond:

1. "Let's look at the idea itself, not just its source."

2. "Where something comes from doesn't always tell the whole story."

3. "The source isn't the only thing that matters—let's check the facts!"

Remember This:

Where something starts doesn't always decide how good or bad it is. Take the time to think about the idea itself!

Chapter 32: The Argument from Silence Fallacy

What Is It?

The Argument from Silence fallacy happens when someone assumes something is true or false just because there's no information about it. It's like saying, "Nobody told me I have homework, so there must not be any!" But just because you haven't heard anything doesn't mean something isn't real or true. Sometimes, silence just means there isn't enough information yet.

Here's an Example:

- Kid 1: "Nobody mentioned a test tomorrow, so we must not have one."

- Kid 2: "But that doesn't mean there's no test. Maybe the teacher just forgot to remind us."

Can you see what's tricky here? Kid 1 is deciding there's no test based on no information at all, but Kid 2 knows that silence doesn't prove anything.

Why Is This a Mistake?

Silence doesn't mean something is true or false—it just means nobody has said anything about it. Making assumptions based on no information can lead to confusion or wrong decisions.

Why Do People Do This?

- They feel impatient and want to fill in the blanks.

- They think that no news must mean something specific.

- They don't realize that silence often means there's not enough information yet.

How to Avoid This Mistake

1. **Wait for More Facts:** Give yourself time to find out the truth before deciding.

2. **Ask Questions:** Try to find evidence instead of making guesses.

3. **Be Comfortable Not Knowing:** It's okay to admit when you don't have all the answers yet.

Practice Example

Let's try!

- Kid 1: "Nobody said I can't bring toys to class, so it must be okay!"

- You: "But that doesn't mean it's allowed. Let's check the class rules to be sure."

How to Handle the Argument from Silence Fallacy

If someone tries to make a point based on no information, you can say:

1. "Just because no one mentioned it doesn't mean it's true or false."

2. "Let's look for real proof instead of guessing."

3. "Sometimes silence just means we don't know yet."

Remember This:

Silence doesn't give you an answer. Not knowing is okay — what matters is finding the facts before making up your mind.

Chapter 33: The Appeal to Probability Fallacy

What Is It?

The Appeal to Probability fallacy happens when someone says something *will* happen just because it *could* happen. It's like saying, "It's possible I'll find money on the ground today, so I definitely will!" Sure, it could happen, but that doesn't mean it's guaranteed. Possibility and certainty are not the same thing.

Here's an Example:

- Kid 1: "I might win the school raffle, so I'm going to win!"

- Kid 2: "It's great to hope, but just because you could win doesn't mean you definitely will."

What's off here? Kid 1 is treating a possibility like it's a sure thing, but Kid 2 knows that just because something can happen doesn't mean it will.

Why Is This a Mistake?

Thinking that something is certain just because it's possible can lead to disappointment or bad decisions. Life is full of possibilities, but not all of them happen. It's important to look at the chances and be realistic.

Why Do People Do This?

- They confuse "could happen" with "will happen."

- They get excited about something they want and assume it's a sure thing.

- They don't think about other possibilities that might stop it from happening.

How to Avoid This Mistake

1. **Think About the Chances:** Ask yourself, "What are the odds of this actually happening?"

2. **Be Realistic:** Remember that possibilities are not guarantees.

3. **Plan for Different Outcomes:** Hope for the best but be ready for other results too.

Practice Example

Let's try!

- Kid 1: "If I study hard, I'll always get an A!"

- You: "Studying is super important, but sometimes other things, like how hard the test is, can make a difference."

How to Handle the Appeal to Probability Fallacy

If someone assumes something will happen just because it can, you can say:

1. "It's possible, but that doesn't mean it's certain."

2. "Let's look at how likely it is instead of just hoping."

3. "It's smart to plan for all the different ways things might go."

Remember This:

Life is full of possibilities, but not all of them will happen. It's great to dream and hope, but always check the facts and stay realistic!

Chapter 34: The Fallacy of Relative Privation

What Is It?

The Fallacy of Relative Privation happens when someone tries to say a problem doesn't matter just because there's something worse. It's like saying, "Why are you upset about your broken toy when there are kids who don't have toys at all?" Sure, there might be bigger problems, but that doesn't mean smaller ones aren't important too.

Here's an Example:

- Kid 1: "I feel sad because I lost my favorite book."

- Kid 2: "Why are you sad? Some kids don't even have books!"

See what's happening? Kid 2 is ignoring Kid 1's feelings by pointing out something else. Just because there are bigger problems doesn't mean Kid 1's feelings don't matter.

Why Is This a Mistake?

Every problem deserves attention, no matter how small it seems. Comparing problems can make people feel like their concerns don't matter, which isn't fair or helpful.

Why Do People Do This?

- They think focusing on bigger problems is more important.

- They might not know how to help with smaller problems.

- They don't realize that all problems, big or small, are important to the person facing them.

How to Avoid This Mistake

1. **Listen First:** Pay attention to the problem without comparing it to others.

2. **Show Empathy:** Remember that everyone's struggles matter.

3. **Help Where You Can:** Focus on solving the problem instead of dismissing it.

Practice Example

Let's try!

- Kid 1: "I'm upset because I got a bad grade on my test."

- You: "I understand why you're upset. Let's think about how to improve next time!"

How to Handle the Fallacy of Relative Privation

If someone dismisses your problem by saying it's small, you can say:

1. "Just because something is smaller doesn't mean it's not important."

2. "All problems matter to the person dealing with them."

3. "We can care about both big and small problems!"

Remember This:

Big problems don't cancel out smaller ones. Everyone's feelings and challenges are important and deserve care and attention.

Chapter 35: The Appeal to Force Fallacy

What Is It?

The Appeal to Force fallacy happens when someone tries to win an argument by threatening or scaring you instead of giving good reasons. It's like saying, "If you don't agree with me, I won't invite you to my party!" Threats might make someone agree, but they don't make the argument true or fair.

Here's an Example:

- Kid 1: "You have to let me go first, or I won't play with you anymore!"

- Kid 2: "That's not fair! Give me a real reason why you should go first."

See the problem? Kid 1 is using a threat to get what they want instead of giving a good reason.

Why Is This a Mistake?

Arguments should be based on facts and fairness, not fear or threats. Using force or intimidation doesn't make someone's point right—it just pressures others to agree.

Why Do People Do This?

- They don't have strong reasons, so they rely on threats.

- They want to control the situation.

- They think fear is the fastest way to win an argument.

How to Avoid This Mistake

1. **Stay Calm:** Don't let fear make your decisions.

2. **Ask for Reasons:** Say, "Can you explain why instead of threatening me?"

3. **Stand Up for Fairness:** Don't give in to threats—focus on what's right.

Practice Example

Let's try!

- Kid 1: "If you don't give me your toy, I'll tell everyone you're mean!"

- You: "That's not a fair reason. Let's figure out how to share instead."

How to Handle the Appeal to Force Fallacy

If someone uses threats, you can respond:

1. "Threats don't make something right — let's talk about it."

2. "You're scaring me, but that doesn't mean I agree."

3. "Let's solve this fairly without using force."

Remember This:

Fair arguments don't use fear or force. Stick to facts and fairness, and don't let threats decide what's right.

Speech bubble (X): "You're so cool, you'll totally agree with me!"

Speech bubble (✓): "Thanks, but let's talk about why your idea works."

Chapter 36: The Appeal to Flattery Fallacy

What Is It?

The Appeal to Flattery fallacy happens when someone tries to convince you by saying something nice instead of giving a good reason. It's like saying, "You're so smart, so you should do my homework for me!" Compliments are great, but they don't make a bad argument true.

Here's an Example:

- Kid 1: "You're the fastest runner in school! Can you clean up for me since you're so good at everything?"

- Kid 2: "Thanks for the compliment, but I'm not doing your clean-up."

What's tricky here? Kid 1 is using flattery to get help, but Kid 2 knows that being complimented doesn't mean they have to agree.

Why Is This a Mistake?

Flattery can feel good, but it doesn't replace real reasons. Using compliments to convince someone can be sneaky and unfair.

Why Do People Do This?

- They think being nice will get them what they want.

- They don't have a strong argument, so they try to charm you instead.

- They hope you won't notice that the compliment isn't related to the request.

How to Avoid This Mistake

1. **Enjoy the Compliment:** Say thank you, but think carefully about the request.

2. **Check the Argument:** Ask, "Does the compliment have anything to do with what they're asking?"

3. **Stick to the Facts:** Don't agree just because of flattery— look for real reasons.

Practice Example

Let's try!

- Kid 1: "You're so good at drawing! Can you do my art project for me?"

- You: "Thanks, but I think you should do your project yourself to learn!"

How to Handle the Appeal to Flattery Fallacy

If someone uses flattery, you can say:

1. "Thanks for the compliment, but what's the real reason?"

2. "Being nice doesn't change what's fair."

3. "I appreciate that, but let's focus on the actual argument."

Remember This:

Compliments are nice, but they don't make a bad argument true. Always think carefully before agreeing!

Chapter 37: The False Attribution Fallacy

What Is It?

The False Attribution fallacy happens when someone uses the name of an expert, source, or fact to make their argument seem true — even if that source isn't reliable or doesn't actually support their point. It's like saying, "This book says dogs can talk, so it must be true!" Just because something sounds official doesn't mean it's accurate.

Here's an Example:

- Kid 1: "I read on a blog that eating only candy is healthy!"

- Kid 2: "Just because a blog said it doesn't mean it's true. Let's check with a doctor or a reliable source."

What's wrong here? Kid 1 is trusting a random source without checking if it's reliable. Kid 2 knows it's important to double-check where the information comes from.

Why Is This a Mistake?

Not all sources can be trusted. If you believe something just because it sounds fancy or important, you could end up believing or sharing something that isn't true.

Why Do People Do This?

- They think attaching a name or source makes their argument stronger.

- They don't check if the source is actually reliable.

- They want to make their argument sound more convincing.

How to Avoid This Mistake

1. **Check the Source:** Ask, "Is this source trustworthy and accurate?"

2. **Look for Proof:** See if other reliable sources agree.

3. **Don't Be Fooled by Names:** Just because something sounds official doesn't mean it's true.

Practice Example:

Let's try!

- Kid 1: "This magazine said unicorns are real!"

- You: "That sounds fun, but let's check if other reliable sources agree."

How to Handle the False Attribution Fallacy

If someone uses a source that doesn't seem reliable, you can say:

1. "Let's check if this source is trustworthy."

2. "Can we find more reliable information to back this up?"

3. "Not all sources are accurate — let's dig deeper."

Remember This:

Not all sources can be trusted. Make sure to double-check information, even if it sounds fancy or important — it might not be true!

Chapter 38: The Broken Window Fallacy

What Is It?

The Broken Window fallacy happens when someone thinks a bad event is actually good because it creates something new. It's like saying, "It's good that the window broke because now we get to fix it!" Fixing the window might help, but the breaking part was still bad!

Here's an Example:

- Kid 1: "It's great that my bike tire popped because now I'll get a new one!"

- Kid 2: "Getting a new tire is helpful, but it would've been better if the tire hadn't popped at all."

What's tricky here? Kid 1 is focusing only on the good thing that came afterward, but Kid 2 knows it's better to avoid the bad thing in the first place.

Why Is This a Mistake?

Bad events don't become good just because something positive happens later. It's important to look at the whole picture, not just the outcome.

Why Do People Do This?

- They want to focus on the positive side of a bad situation.

- They forget that the bad event wasn't necessary for the good thing to happen.

- They confuse the result with the cause.

How to Avoid This Mistake

1. **Think About the Cause:** Ask, "Was the bad event really needed for this good thing to happen?"

2. **Separate the Bad and Good:** Focus on how to avoid bad events while still finding solutions.

3. **Look at the Bigger Picture:** Don't let the outcome overshadow the original problem.

Practice Example

Let's try!

- Kid 1: "It's great that I spilled my juice because now I get a new cup!"

- You: "Getting a new cup is nice, but it's better to avoid spilling the juice in the first place."

How to Handle the Broken Window Fallacy

If someone says a bad event is good because of what comes after, you can say:

1. "The good outcome doesn't erase the bad event."

2. "Let's focus on how to avoid the bad event next time."

3. "It's great to find solutions, but the problem is still a problem."

Remember This:

Good things can come after bad events, but that doesn't make the bad event good. Always look at the full story!

Chapter 39: The Appeal to Common Sense Fallacy

What Is It?

The Appeal to Common Sense fallacy happens when someone says something must be true just because it sounds obvious. It's like saying, "Everyone knows this is the right answer!" But sometimes, what feels obvious isn't actually true, and you need real evidence to back it up.

Here's an Example:

- Kid 1: "It's common sense that plants grow faster if you talk to them!"

- Kid 2: "That sounds interesting, but let's look for proof to see if it's really true."

See the problem? Kid 1 is relying on what "everyone knows," but Kid 2 knows it's important to check if the idea is actually true.

Why Is This a Mistake?

Not everything that seems obvious is correct. Assuming something is true just because it feels right can stop you from finding the real facts.

Why Do People Do This?

- They trust their instincts without checking the facts.

- They think if an idea is popular, it must be true.

- They don't realize that "common sense" can be wrong.

How to Avoid This Mistake

1. **Ask for Evidence:** Say, "What proof do we have for this?"

2. **Think Critically:** Don't assume something is true just because it feels right.

3. **Look for Facts:** Check if the idea is supported by real information.

Practice Example

Let's try!

- Kid 1: "It's common sense that cold weather makes you sick!"

- You: "Cold weather feels bad, but let's check if it really causes sickness."

How to Handle the Appeal to Common Sense Fallacy

If someone says something is true because it's "obvious," you can say:

1. "Just because it seems obvious doesn't mean it's true — let's check it out."

2. "What feels right might not always be right — let's look for proof."

3. "Common sense is a good guess, but facts are what really matter."

Remember This:

Just because something feels obvious doesn't mean it's correct. Take a moment to check the facts and think it through before making up your mind!

Chapter 40: The False Balance Fallacy

What Is It?

The False Balance fallacy happens when someone treats two sides of an argument as if they're equally true or valid — even when one side clearly has stronger evidence. It's like saying, "Let's hear both sides: the idea that the Earth is round and the idea that it's flat." Sure, everyone can have an opinion, but not all opinions are backed by facts.

Here's an Example:

- Kid 1: "Some people say eating only candy is healthy!"

- Kid 2: "Just because some people say that doesn't mean it's as true as eating fruits and veggies!"

Can you spot the mistake? Kid 1 is giving equal weight to two ideas, even though one has much stronger evidence. Kid 2 knows that facts should matter more than just opinions.

Why Is This a Mistake?

Not all ideas are equally true or backed by evidence. Treating them as if they are can confuse people and make bad ideas seem better than they are.

Why Do People Do This?

- They want to be fair and let both sides share their ideas.

- They don't know that one side might have more proof than the other.

- They think all opinions are equally true, even when some don't have facts to back them up.

How to Avoid This Mistake

1. **Check the Evidence:** Ask, "Which side has more facts to back it up?"

2. **Don't Confuse Opinions with Facts:** Remember, just because someone says something doesn't make it true.

3. **Be Fair but Smart:** Listening to both sides is good, but facts should decide what's right.

Practice Example

Let's try!

- Kid 1: "Some people think you don't need to wear a helmet when riding a bike."

- You: "That's their opinion, but the facts show helmets keep us safer, so we should wear them!"

How to Handle the False Balance Fallacy

If someone treats two sides as equally true when they're not, you can say:

1. "Let's check which side has stronger evidence."

2. "Opinions are fine, but facts are what matter most."

3. "It's okay to listen to both sides, but the truth isn't always in the middle."

Remember This:

Being fair doesn't mean all ideas are equally true. Always look for the facts and let the strongest evidence guide your thinking!

Chapter 41–50: Advanced Fallacies (Made Easy!)

Hey there, logical thinker! You're doing amazing so far! This section is like leveling up in a game — here, you'll learn about some tricky fallacies that can fool even the smartest people. Don't worry, though! We'll break everything down and keep it fun, so you'll know how to spot these sneaky tricks.

Chapter 41: The Just-World Fallacy

What Is It?

The Just-World fallacy happens when someone believes that life is always fair — like thinking, "Good things only happen to good people, and bad things only happen to bad people." But life doesn't always work that way. Sometimes, bad things happen to good people, and good things happen to people who don't deserve them.

Here's an Example:

- Kid 1: "That kid got detention — they must have done something bad."

- Kid 2: "Maybe, but it's also possible they didn't do anything wrong. Let's find out what happened."

What's happening here? Kid 1 is assuming that life is balanced for everyone, but Kid 2 knows that sometimes people get into trouble even when it's not their fault. It's not always about who deserves what — it could be about something else entirely.

Why Is This a Mistake?

Believing that the world is perfect can make you miss the bigger picture. Sometimes things happen because of bad luck, mistakes, or circumstances that are out of anyone's control.

Why Do People Do This?

- They want to feel safe, thinking bad things only happen if someone deserves it.

- It's easier to blame someone than to think about other reasons for what happened.

- Believing life is fair makes the world feel more predictable.

How to Avoid This Mistake

1. **Ask Questions:** Instead of assuming, ask, "What else could explain this?"

2. **Think About Luck:** Remember that bad luck can happen to anyone, even if they didn't do anything wrong.

3. **Be Kind:** Instead of blaming, think about how you can help or understand the situation better.

Practice Example

Let's try!

- Kid 1: "That kid fell off their bike because they're clumsy."

- You: "Maybe, or maybe they hit a rock they didn't see."

How to Handle the Just-World Fallacy

If someone says something unfair because they believe the world is always just, you can say:

1. "Sometimes bad things happen to good people — it's not their fault."

2. "Let's think about other reasons why this could have happened."

3. "Life isn't always fair, but we can still try to make it better."

Remember This:

The world isn't flawless, and that's okay. What matters is looking for the real reasons behind what happens and being kind to others. Understanding this can help you be more compassionate and a better problem-solver!

Chapter 42: The Ludic Fallacy

What Is It?

The Ludic Fallacy happens when someone assumes that life works like a game, where every rule is clear and every outcome is predictable. But life isn't always that simple! In real life, unexpected things can happen, and not everything follows a set of rules.

Here's an Example:

- Kid 1: "If I practice soccer for one hour every day, I'll definitely become a pro!"

- Kid 2: "Practice is great, but other things, like teamwork and opportunities, matter too."

See the problem? Kid 1 thinks life works like a step-by-step guide, but Kid 2 knows there's more to it.

Why Is This a Mistake?

Thinking life is like a game can make you miss out on surprises or other important factors. Life is messy and full of unknowns. Believing everything is predictable can lead to wrong expectations or disappointment.

Why Do People Do This?

- They like things to be neat and simple.
- They believe following the "rules" always leads to success.
- They want to feel in control of outcomes.

How to Avoid This Mistake

1. **Expect the Unexpected:** Remember, life doesn't always follow the rules you expect.

2. **Look at the Bigger Picture:** Think about all the factors that might affect a situation.

3. **Stay Flexible:** Be ready to adjust when things don't go as planned.

Practice Example

Let's try!

- Kid 1: "If I wear my lucky socks, I'll win the game!"
- You: "Maybe, but practicing and working as a team are what really help us win."

How to Handle the Ludic Fallacy

If someone thinks life works like a game, you can say:

1. "Life's not always that simple — let's think about what else could happen."

2. "There's more to life than following one rule."

3. "It's great to have a plan, but we also need to stay flexible."

Remember This:

Life isn't a game, and that's okay! Being open to surprises and thinking about all the possibilities helps you handle whatever comes your way.

Chapter 43: The Pro-Innovation Bias Fallacy

What Is It?

The Pro-Innovation Bias happens when someone thinks new things are always better, just because they're new. It's like thinking, "This new game is the best ever!" without checking if it's actually fun or better than the old one.

Here's an Example:

- Kid 1: "This new toy must be the best—it just came out!"

- Kid 2: "Let's try it first to see if it's actually better than what we already have."

What's happening? Kid 1 is overly excited about something new, but Kid 2 knows it's important to test it out before deciding if it's really better.

Why Is This a Mistake?

Not everything new is better. Sometimes, old things work just as well! Judging something only by how new it is can make you miss out on other important details, like how useful or fun it really is.

Why Do People Do This?

- They think new means exciting and better.

- They like being the first to try something.

- They believe old things are always worse.

How to Avoid This Mistake

1. **Ask Questions:** Think, "Is this better, or just newer?"

2. **Test It Out:** Try new things, but don't forget to compare them to what you already know works.

3. **Don't Judge Too Quickly:** Give old things a chance before tossing them aside.

Practice Example

Let's try!

- Kid 1: "This new marker set must be better than the old one!"

- You: "Let's try it first and see if it works better."

How to Handle the Pro-Innovation Bias

If someone is overly excited about something new, you can say:

1. "New doesn't always mean better — let's check it out first."

2. "What makes it better than what we already have?"

3. "Trying new things is fun, but it's smart to see if it really works."

Remember This:

It's fun to explore new ideas and things, but don't forget to think about how they compare to what already works. Not everything shiny and new is better!

Chapter 44: The Halo Effect Fallacy

What Is It?

The Halo Effect happens when you think everything about a person or thing is amazing, just because one part of it is great. It's like saying, "She's good at soccer, so she must be good at math too!" But being awesome at one thing doesn't automatically make someone great at everything else.

Here's an Example:

- Kid 1: "This candy tastes amazing! I bet it's super healthy too."

- Kid 2: "Just because it tastes good doesn't mean it's good for you!"

See the mistake? Kid 1 assumes one good thing (the taste) makes everything about the candy good. But Kid 2 knows better.

Why Is This a Mistake?

When you let one good thing create a "halo," it can cloud your judgment. You might miss the not-so-great stuff, like candy being unhealthy or a good soccer player not being great at math. It's important to look at the whole picture, not just the shiny parts.

Why Do People Do This?

- They focus on the good stuff and ignore the bad.

- They want to believe something is perfect.

- It's easier to make a quick judgment than to think deeply.

How to Avoid This Mistake:

1. **Look Closer:** Ask yourself, "Is everything about this really amazing?"

2. **Separate the Parts:** Think about each part on its own instead of letting one good thing take over.

3. **Stay Curious:** Don't assume—ask questions to find the truth.

Practice Example

Let's try!

- Kid 1: "She's the best soccer player! I bet she's the smartest too."

- You: "Being good at soccer is great, but let's see how she does in other things first."

How to Handle the Halo Effect Fallacy

If someone is dazzled by one good thing, you can say:

1. "That part is awesome, but let's think about the other stuff too."

2. "What makes you think everything else is just as great?"

3. "It's okay to like something, but let's not ignore the facts."

Remember This:

One great thing doesn't make everything great. Keep your eyes open and think about the big picture. That way, you'll always make smarter choices!

Chapter 45: The Planning Fallacy

What Is It?

The Planning Fallacy happens when you think something will be faster or easier than it really is. It's like saying, "I'll clean my whole room in 10 minutes!" and then realizing it takes way longer because you keep finding toys to play with.

Here's an Example:

- Kid 1: "This art project will take me just an hour to finish!"

- Kid 2: "Are you sure? Don't forget you need time to draw, paint, and let it dry!"

What's going on? Kid 1 underestimates how much time the project will really take, but Kid 2 knows there's more to the task than it seems.

Why Is This a Mistake?

If you don't plan properly, you might run out of time or get overwhelmed. Big projects, like homework or cleaning, often have extra steps you don't think about at first.

Why Do People Do This?

- They focus on the easy parts and forget the tricky ones.
- They want to get started quickly without thinking it through.
- They feel excited and underestimate the effort needed.

How to Avoid This Mistake

1. **Break It Down:** Think about all the steps and how long each one will take.
2. **Add Extra Time:** Give yourself a little more time than you think you need.
3. **Ask for Help:** If you're not sure, ask someone who's done it before.

Practice Example

Let's try!

- Kid 1: "I can finish this puzzle before dinner!"
- You: "That's cool, but don't forget to count how many pieces there are!"

How to Handle the Planning Fallacy

If someone thinks a task will be quick and easy, you can say:

1. "Let's list out all the steps — it might take longer than you think."

2. "It's better to plan for more time than to run out!"

3. "Getting things done well is more important than rushing."

Remember This:

Good planning takes time! If you think through all the steps and give yourself extra time, you'll finish your tasks without stress—and maybe even have fun doing them.

Chapter 46: The Self-Sealing Fallacy

What Is It?

The Self-Sealing Fallacy happens when someone makes an argument that can't be proven wrong, no matter what. They keep changing the rules or the argument to make it impossible to disagree. It's like saying, "If I win, it's because I'm awesome, and if I lose, it's because the game was unfair!"

Here's an Example:

- Kid 1: "I'm the fastest runner!"

- Kid 2: "But I just beat you in a race."

- Kid 1: "That doesn't count because I wasn't trying my best!"

What's going on? Kid 1 keeps changing the rules to protect their argument. No matter what Kid 2 says, Kid 1 finds a way to stay "right."

Why Is This a Mistake?

Arguments like this can't be proven or tested because the person keeps shifting the goalposts. It's not fair, and it makes it hard to have a real conversation or figure out the truth.

Why Do People Do This?

- They don't want to admit they might be wrong.

- They think changing the argument makes them look smarter.

- They want to win at all costs.

How to Avoid This Mistake

1. **Stick to One Idea:** Make your point clear and don't keep changing it.

2. **Be Open to Feedback:** If someone challenges your argument, think about what they're saying.

3. **Respect the Rules:** Don't bend the argument just to stay right.

Practice Example

Let's try!

- Kid 1: "I'm great at drawing!"

- Kid 2: "But you didn't win the art contest."

- Kid 1: "That's because the judges don't know good art!"

How to Handle the Self-Sealing Fallacy

If someone keeps changing their argument, you can say:

1. "Can we agree on one idea and stick to it?"

2. "It's okay to be wrong sometimes — it helps us learn!"

3. "Let's focus on what we can both agree on."

Remember This:

Changing the rules to always be right isn't right. The best way to grow and learn is by listening to others and being honest about what's true!

Chapter 47: The Misleading Vividness Fallacy

What Is It?

The Misleading Vividness Fallacy happens when one dramatic example is used to make a point, even if it's not common or likely. It's like saying, "We shouldn't eat apples because one kid once choked on one!" That's scary, but it doesn't mean apples are bad for everyone.

Here's an Example:

- Kid 1: "Don't ride bikes —my cousin fell off and got hurt!"

- Kid 2: "That's sad, but lots of kids ride bikes safely every day."

Spotted the mistake? Kid 1 is using one scary story to argue against biking, but Kid 2 knows that one example doesn't tell the whole story.

Why Is This a Mistake?

Big, scary stories can stick in your head, but they don't always show what usually happens. If you focus on just one vivid example, you might ignore the facts or the bigger picture.

Why Do People Do This?

- Scary or exciting stories are easier to remember than boring facts.

- They want to grab attention and make their argument sound stronger.

- They don't realize one example isn't enough to prove a point.

How to Avoid This Mistake

1. **Look at the Bigger Picture:** Think about how often something actually happens.

2. **Check the Facts:** Don't rely on one example—find more information.

3. **Stay Calm:** Don't let scary stories make you forget the truth.

Practice Example

Let's try!

- Kid 1: "Don't go swimming — there was a shark attack on TV!"

- You: "Shark attacks are super rare. Let's learn how to swim safely instead."

How to Handle the Misleading Vividness Fallacy

If someone uses a dramatic example to make a point, you can say:

1. "That's one story, but does it happen a lot?"

2. "Let's see what the facts say about this."

3. "It's important to think about what usually happens, not just one time."

Remember This:

Exciting or scary stories can grab your attention, but they don't always show the full truth. Facts and patterns are better tools for making smart choices!

Chapter 48: The False Consensus Effect

What Is It?

The False Consensus Effect happens when someone thinks that most people agree with them, even if they don't. It's like saying, "Everyone loves pineapple on pizza because I do!" But wait — have they asked everyone?

Here's an Example:

- Kid 1: "Everyone at school agrees my team should win!"

- Kid 2: "Did you ask everyone, or just your friends?"

What's happening? Kid 1 assumes everyone thinks the same way they do, but Kid 2 knows that's not how opinions work.

Why Is This a Mistake?

It's easy to think your opinion is super popular because it feels right to you. But not everyone sees things the same way, and assuming they do can lead to bad decisions.

Why Do People Do This?

- They spend time with people who think like them, so it feels like "everyone" agrees.

- They don't stop to think that other people might have different ideas.

- It's easier to assume agreement than to ask for opinions.

How to Avoid This Mistake

1. **Ask Around:** Don't assume—find out what others actually think.

2. **Be Open to Differences:** Understand that not everyone sees things your way.

3. **Check the Facts:** Use evidence instead of guessing how popular an idea is.

Practice Example

Let's try!

- Kid 1: "Everyone loves this band—they're the best!"

- You: "I don't like them much. Maybe not *everyone* agrees with you!"

How to Handle the False Consensus Effect

If someone assumes everyone agrees with them, you can say:

1. "That's what you think, but have you asked other people?"

2. "Just because you like it doesn't mean everyone does."

3. "It's okay if people have different favorites — that's what makes things fun!"

Remember This:

Not everyone sees the world the same way, and that's okay! It's important to listen and learn from others instead of assuming everyone agrees with you.

Chapter 49: The Argument from Repetition (Ad Nauseam) Fallacy

What Is It?

The Argument from Repetition happens when someone repeats an idea over and over to make it seem true. It's like saying, "If I say it enough, everyone will believe me!" But repeating something doesn't make it right.

Here's an Example:

- Kid 1: "I'm the best at basketball!"

- Kid 2: "You've said that a hundred times, but you still miss most of your shots!"

What's going on? Kid 1 keeps repeating their claim, but Kid 2 knows that saying it over and over doesn't make it true.

Why Is This a Mistake?

Repetition can make an idea feel more familiar, but it doesn't prove it's right. A good argument needs facts, not just lots of talking.

Why Do People Do This?

- They think saying something enough will make people believe it.

- They don't have strong facts, so they rely on repetition.

- They hope others will stop questioning them if they hear it often.

How to Avoid This Mistake

1. **Use Facts, Not Repetition:** Share evidence, not just the same words.

2. **Listen to Others:** Don't keep repeating—hear what they have to say.

3. **Stay Open-Minded:** Be ready to change your mind if the facts don't match.

Practice Example:

Let's try!

- Kid 1: "This toy is the coolest! This toy is the coolest!"

- You: "Why do you think it's the coolest? Can you explain?"

How to Handle the Argument from Repetition:

If someone keeps repeating themselves, you can say:

1. "You've said that already — what's your reason?"

2. "Repeating doesn't make it true—can we look at the facts?"

3. "Let's talk about why you think that instead of just saying it again."

Remember This:

Saying something over and over doesn't make it true. Good arguments need strong evidence, not just lots of words!

Chapter 50: Poisoning the Well

What Is It?

Poisoning the Well happens when someone tries to make you dislike or mistrust someone else's argument before you even hear it. It's like saying, "Don't listen to her — she doesn't know anything!" before she's even had a chance to speak. This fallacy is like putting a big "Don't trust this person!" sign in front of someone, which isn't fair at all.

Here's an Example:

- Kid 1: "Don't listen to Sam — he never tells the truth!"

- Sam: "Hey, that's not true! You haven't even heard what I have to say yet!"

What's happening here? Kid 1 is trying to make everyone doubt Sam before Sam has even started talking. That's Poisoning the

Well! It distracts people from the actual idea and focuses on making someone look bad instead.

Why Is This a Mistake?

This is a mistake because it's unfair to judge someone's ideas before hearing them out. Imagine if someone said nobody should listen to your idea just because they don't like you—that wouldn't feel good, would it? By dismissing someone before they get a chance to speak, we might miss out on something smart or helpful.

Why Do People Do This?

- **They're scared of losing the argument:** If the other person has a good point, they try to stop others from listening to it.

- **It's easier than explaining their own ideas:** They'd rather attack the person than focus on the argument.

- **They want to control the conversation:** By making others look bad, they hope people will only listen to them.

How to Avoid This Mistake

1. **Listen first:** Always hear what someone has to say before deciding if it's good or bad.

2. **Talk about ideas, not people:** Focus on the message, not who's delivering it.

3. **Stay open-minded:** Give everyone a fair chance to share their thoughts without pre-judging.

Practice Example

Let's try!

- Kid 1: "Don't listen to Emma — she's always wrong!"

- You: "Let's hear what Emma has to say first. Everyone deserves a chance."

How to Handle Poisoning the Well

If someone tries to dismiss an idea before you've even heard it, here's what you can do:

1. **Stay neutral:** "Let's be fair and listen before we decide."

2. **Point out the unfairness:** "It's not right to judge without hearing their idea."

3. **Encourage fairness:** "I'd like to hear both sides before making up my mind."

Remember This:

Judging someone before they speak is like closing a book before reading the first page. You might miss out on something amazing! Ideas should be judged on what they are, not who they come from. Give everyone a fair chance, and you'll always be closer to the truth.

Conclusion: Thinking Clearly in a World of Silly Arguments!

Congratulations, logical thinker! You've just completed a big journey through the world of tricky arguments and sneaky fallacies. Now, you're ready to use your new superpower — clear thinking!

The world is full of people trying to persuade you of all sorts of things. Some will be fair, and others might try to confuse you. But don't worry — you've got the tools to spot silly arguments, ask smart questions, and focus on what really matters.

Always remember:

- **Be Curious:** Ask questions and dig deeper. The truth loves a curious mind!

- **Be Fair:** Listen to others and consider their ideas, even if you don't agree at first.

- **Be Brave:** Don't be afraid to say, "Wait a second, that doesn't make sense!" when something feels off.

You're now a champion of clear thinking, ready to handle tricky debates, tricky ideas, and even your everyday conversations. The world needs more people like you—people who think with their heads and their hearts. So, go ahead, use your skills, and make smarter decisions. You're ready to shine!

Appendix A: Quick Reference Guide to Logical Fallacies

Use this list for a quick reminder of each fallacy. This quick guide makes it easy to recall and detect fallacies anytime!

1. **Ad Hominem:** Attacking the person instead of the idea.

   "You're wrong because you're too young!"

2. **Straw Man:** Misrepresenting someone's argument to make it easier to attack.

   "You want us to never eat candy again? That's too extreme!"

3. **False Dilemma:** Pretending there are only two choices when there are more.

   "It's my way or the highway!"

4. **Bandwagon:** Believing something is true because everyone else does.

   "Everyone says this game is the best, so it must be true!"

---

5. **Appeal to Authority:** Assuming something is true just because an expert says so.

   "The CEO said it's great, so it must be!"

6. **Appeal to Emotion:** Using feelings instead of facts to persuade.

   "If you don't agree, you'll make everyone sad!"

7. **Hasty Generalization:** Jumping to a conclusion without enough evidence.

   "All cats are mean because my cat scratched me!"

8. **Slippery Slope:** Saying one small thing will lead to a big disaster.

   "If we allow one cookie before dinner, we'll eat junk food forever!"

9. **Red Herring:** Distracting from the topic with something unrelated.

   "We're talking about homework, not my messy room!"

10. **Circular Reasoning:** Using the conclusion as proof of itself.

    "I'm right because I said so!"

11. **Loaded Question:** Asking a question that traps the other person.

    "Why are you always so lazy?"

12. **Gambler's Fallacy:** Believing past events affect future outcomes.

    "This coin has landed on heads three times—it's due for tails!"

13. **Appeal to Tradition:** Thinking something is right because it's old or traditional.

   "We've always done it this way, so it must be best!"

14. **Sunk Cost Fallacy:** Sticking with something because you've already invested in it.

   "I can't quit now—I've already spent so much time on it!"

15. **Middle Ground:** Assuming the truth is somewhere between two extremes.

   "Maybe the Earth is kind of round and kind of flat."

16. **Cherry Picking:** Only using the facts that support your argument.

   "Look! This one piece of data proves I'm right!"

17. **Appeal to Nature:** Believing something is better because it's natural.

   "This snack is natural, so it must be healthy!"

18. **Appeal to Consequences:** Judging something as true or false based on its effects.

   "If this is true, it would be bad—so it can't be true!"

19. **Personal Incredulity:** Thinking something isn't true because it's hard to understand.

   "I don't get how this works, so it must be fake!"

20. **Appeal to Novelty:** Believing something is better because it's new.

   "This gadget is new, so it's the best!"

21. **No True Scotsman:** Changing the rules of a group to exclude someone.

"No real soccer fan would like that team!"

22. **Texas Sharpshooter:** Only focusing on information that supports your argument.

    "These three wins prove I'm the best!"

23. **Survivorship Bias:** Ignoring the failures and only looking at successes.

    "If they made it big, so can anyone!"

24. **Scare Tactic:** Using fear to win an argument instead of facts.

    "If you don't agree, something terrible will happen!"

25. **Appeal to Personal Experience:** Thinking your own story proves everything.

    "I've seen it happen, so it must be true for everyone!"

26. **Composition Fallacy:** Assuming the whole is good because the parts are good.

    "All these puzzle pieces look great, so the picture must be amazing!"

27. **Division Fallacy:** Assuming every part is true because the whole is true.

    "This cake is delicious, so every ingredient must taste good!"

28. **Appeal to Hypocrisy:** Dodging the argument by pointing out someone else's flaws.

    "You can't tell me to clean up—you're messy too!"

29. **Appeal to Pity:** Using sympathy to win instead of evidence.

"You should let me go first because I had a bad day."

30. **False Equivalence:** Treating two unequal things as if they're the same.

    "Cats and fish are the same—they're both pets!"

31. **Genetic Fallacy:** Judging something based on where it came from.

    "That idea came from him, so it must be bad."

32. **Argument from Silence:** Thinking no evidence means something isn't true.

    "If no one said it, it must not be real."

33. **Appeal to Probability:** Believing something will happen just because it could.

    "It's possible, so it's definitely going to happen!"

34. **Fallacy of Relative Privation:** Saying one problem isn't important because there's a bigger problem.

    "Why care about your broken toy? Some kids have no toys!"

35. **Appeal to Force:** Using threats instead of reasons to persuade.

    "You'd better agree, or else!"

36. **Appeal to Flattery:** Using compliments to win someone over.

    "You're so smart—don't you agree with me?"

37. **False Attribution:** Believing something is true just because an unreliable source said so.

    "A random website said it, so it must be true!"

38. **Broken Window Fallacy:** Thinking damage is good because it creates jobs to fix it.

   "Breaking stuff helps the economy!"

39. **Appeal to Common Sense:** Saying something must be true because it seems obvious.

   "It's common sense—why question it?"

40. **False Balance:** Treating two sides as equal even when one has better evidence.

   "Let's give both opinions the same weight, even if one is weaker."

41. **Just-World Fallacy:** Believing the world is always fair.

   "If something bad happened, they must have deserved it."

42. **Ludic Fallacy:** Assuming real life works like a game or simulation.

   "I won this video game, so I can do the same in real life!"

43. **Pro-Innovation Bias:** Thinking new things are always better.

   "This new gadget must be the best!"

44. **Halo Effect:** Letting one good trait influence your judgment on everything else.

   "They're good at art, so they must be great at math too!"

45. **Planning Fallacy:** Underestimating how long something will take.

   "We'll finish this project in one hour—easy!"

46. **Self-Sealing Fallacy:** Making an argument impossible to prove wrong.

"If you don't agree, you just don't understand!"

47. **Misleading Vividness:** Using one dramatic example to make a big claim.

    "That one accident proves flying is unsafe!"

48. **False Consensus Effect:** Believing everyone thinks the same as you.

    "Everyone loves this book—it's the best!"

49. **Argument from Repetition:** Thinking something is true just because it's repeated.

    "I've told you this ten times, so it must be true!"

50. **Poisoning the Well:** Discrediting someone before they even speak.

    "Don't listen to them—they're always wrong!"

Appendix B: Practice Scenarios for Kids (Spot the Fallacy Game!)

Below are 15 fun and engaging scenarios for you to figure out which fallacy is being used. Read each one carefully, and then check the answers at the end of this section to see if you're a fallacy detective!

---

1. The Movie Star Expert

Kid 1: "This toothpaste is the best because a famous actor said so!"

Kid 2: "What does acting have to do with toothpaste?"

What's the fallacy?

---

2. The Mean Math Teacher

Kid 1: "Our math teacher says 2+2=4, but they're so strict! They can't be right."

Kid 2: "But does their personality change the math?"

What's the fallacy?

---

3. The Ultimate Toy Debate

Kid 1: "Either you like this toy, or you don't like fun at all!"

Kid 2: "Wait, can't I like other toys too?"

What's the fallacy?

---

4. The Popular Choice

Kid 1: "Everyone is wearing these shoes, so they must be the best!"

Kid 2: "Does popularity always mean quality?"

What's the fallacy?

---

5. The Candy Catastrophe

Kid 1: "If you eat one candy, you'll end up eating ten and get cavities!"

Kid 2: "That seems like a big leap."

What's the fallacy?

---

6. The Tricky Question

Kid 1: "Why do you always forget to do your chores?"

Kid 2: "Wait, who said I always forget?"

What's the fallacy?

7. The Fancy Professor

Kid 1: "This professor said the moon is made of cheese, so it must be true!"

Kid 2: "Do they have proof for that?"

What's the fallacy?

8. The "Real Fan" Rule

Kid 1: "If you don't watch every game, you're not a real fan of the team."

Kid 2: "Can't I be a fan and miss some games?"

What's the fallacy?

9. The Fear Tactic

Kid 1: "If you don't do your homework, the teacher will yell at you forever!"

Kid 2: "That's a bit extreme."

What's the fallacy?

10. The Puzzle Problem

Kid 1: "All these puzzle pieces are colorful, so the final picture must be beautiful!"

Kid 2: "What if the picture doesn't make sense, even if the pieces are pretty?"

What's the fallacy?

11. The Amazing Athlete

Kid 1: "She's so good at sports, so she must be the best person to help us with math homework!"

Kid 2: "What does sports have to do with math?"

What's the fallacy?

---

12. The Weather Expert

Kid 1: "It hasn't rained all week, so it definitely won't rain tomorrow."

Kid 2: "Is that how weather works?"

What's the fallacy?

---

13. The Big Problem Argument

Kid 1: "Why are you worried about your missing notebook? Some people don't even have school supplies."

Kid 2: "Can't both be problems?"

What's the fallacy?

---

14. The Repeating Rule

Kid 1: "I've told you five times that I'm right, so I must be!"

Kid 2: "Saying it more doesn't make it true."

What's the fallacy?

15. The Garden Argument

Kid 1: "Plants are natural, so they're always good for you."

Kid 2: "What about poison ivy?"

What's the fallacy?

_____

Answers: Spot the Fallacy

1. Appeal to Authority

2. Ad Hominem

3. False Dilemma

4. Bandwagon

5. Slippery Slope

6. Loaded Question

7. Appeal to Authority

8. No True Scotsman

9. Scare Tactic

10. Composition Fallacy

11. Halo Effect

12. Appeal to Probability

13. Fallacy of Relative Privation

14. Argument from Repetition

15. Appeal to Nature

Have fun spotting these fallacies in real life and practice keeping your thinking sharp!

Appendix C: Tips for Debating and Winning Arguments

Debating can be fun and a great way to learn new things. Whether you're talking with your friends, classmates, or even adults, it's important to stay calm, listen carefully, and use good reasoning. Here are some tips to help you debate like a pro and win arguments the smart way:

1. Stay Cool, Stay Kind

- Don't get angry or mean, even if the other person does. People listen better when you stay calm and friendly.

- Remember, winning an argument doesn't mean making someone feel bad — it's about helping them see the truth.

2. Listen Like a Detective

- Pay attention to what the other person says. Are they making any fallacies or mistakes in their argument?

- Ask questions to understand their point of view better, like, "Can you explain why you think that?"

3. Use Facts, Not Feelings

- Base your argument on evidence, research, and logic—not just opinions or emotions.
- Example: Instead of saying, "I feel this is right," say, "Here's why this works: [insert facts]."

4. Ask Good Questions

- Challenge ideas politely by asking questions like:
  - "What's your evidence for that?"
  - "What if things work differently than you think?"
- Questions help others think more clearly and find flaws in their argument.

5. Spot the Fallacies

- Watch out for common mistakes like:
  - "Everyone says it, so it must be true!" (Bandwagon Fallacy)
  - "This is just common sense!" (Appeal to Common Sense Fallacy)
- Politely point out these errors to make your case stronger.

6. Keep It Simple

- Use clear, simple words to explain your point. Don't confuse others with complicated language or too many ideas at once.
- Example: Instead of saying, "This hypothesis is flawed," say, "That idea has some problems."

7. Know When to Stop

- If the other person refuses to listen or keeps getting upset, it's okay to end the debate. You can say, "Let's agree to disagree for now."

- Sometimes, it's better to walk away than to argue forever.

8. Be Open to Learning

- If someone makes a good point, don't be afraid to admit it. Saying, "You're right about that," shows you're fair and willing to learn.

- A good debate isn't about "winning" but finding the truth together.

9. Practice, Practice, Practice

- Try debating with your friends or family on fun topics, like "What's the best pizza topping?" or "Should kids have more recess?"

- The more you practice, the better you'll get at spotting fallacies and explaining your ideas clearly.

10. Stay Curious

- Always be ready to learn something new. Read books, ask questions, and stay curious about the world. The more you know, the stronger your arguments will be!

Final Thought

Debating is like a fun game for your brain. You get to practice thinking, listening, and learning. Even if you don't "win" every argument, you'll grow smarter and more confident every time you try. So keep talking, keep learning, and keep thinking clearly — you've got this!

www.ingramcontent.com/pod-product-compliance
Lightning Source LLC
Chambersburg PA
CBHW070812300326

41914CB00054B/789